Becoming Myself

Becoming Myself

Living Life to the Fullest
After the Loss of Your Parents

Shari Butler, Ph.D.

McGRAW-HILL

New York Chicago San Francisco Lisbon
London Madrid Mexico City Milan New Delhi
San Juan Seoul Singapore Sydney Toronto

The **McGraw·Hill** Companies

1 2 3 4 5 6 7 8 9 0 DOC/DOC 0 9 8 7 6 5 4 3

ISBN 0-07-138766-8

McGraw-Hill books are available at special quantity discounts to use as premiums and sales promotions, or for use in corporate training programs. For more information, please write to the Director of Special Sales, Professional Publishing, McGraw-Hill, Two Penn Plaza, New York, NY 10121-2298. Or contact your local bookstore.

 This book is printed on recycled, acid-free paper containing a minimum of 50% recycled, de-inked fiber.

Library of Congress Cataloging-in-Publication Data

Butler, Shari.
  Becoming myself : living life to the fullest after the loss of your parents / by Shari Butler.—1st ed.
     p. cm.
Includes bibliographical references and index.
  ISBN 0-07-138766-8 (pbk. : alk. paper)
  1. Parents—Death 2. Adult children—Psychology. I. Title.
  HO1073.B88 2003
  155.9'37—dc22
                                    2003015872

I DEDICATE THIS BOOK WITH LOVE TO:

my parents, Faye and Lou Butler,
who are no longer with me;

my brother, Dr. Mel Butler, whose reminders
that I share creative agony with some of
the best artists and writers were a source
of comfort;

my husband, Robert Schrage, who provided
emotional, intellectual, and technical support
and who deserves a medal for bearing this
process with me,

my darling and precious daughter, Alexandra,
whose mind, beauty, grace, wit, and charm
make each day worth living.

Contents

Acknowledgments

There are many people I would like to thank for various reasons. First of all, my dear friend Denise Torv for making connections for me in the publishing world. Then I would like to thank Joelle Delbourgo for her rationality in times of confusion; Nancy Hancock for sharing an inspirational vision with me; Nancy Mandler, a creative comrade; Valerie Hiss for being my lifelong support system and friend; my Aunt Marion and Uncle Bernard Barsky for always telling me things would be fine; Margaret Blackstone, my soul mate and muse, who saved the day more than once; Joyce Robinson, my dear and supportive friend; my East Coast business partner and friend Robert C. Sabin, who builds lovely homes; and Scott Manning, who smiled when I needed it most.

—Shari Butler

1

Rediscovering Yourself

God picks up the reed flute world and blows.
Each note is a need coming through one of us,
A passion, a longing pain . . .
Don't try to end it.
Be your note.
I'll show you how it is enough.
Go upon the roof at night
In this city of the soul . . .
Sing loud!

—*Rumi, twelfth-century Sufi poet*

Whatever unique path you take through the stages of life—from infancy through adolescence and adulthood—you learn, inevitably, that development brings both the excitement and joy of gain and the sorrow and difficulty of loss as part of its very nature. You cannot have one without the other. For each step forward, something is—and *must* be—abandoned. Once you recognize this, you may even embrace it. Knowing that growth will accompany our changes allows some of the shadows to slip away from loss because of the light cast by the gains we make.

Accumulating these losses and gains along the journey, we can come to view some stages of life as being more about one than the other. One person will find that he mourns the passing of his innocence more than he values the awareness that replaces it. Another will regret the slowing of her muscles and the dulling of her quick thinking more than she appreciates the wisdom of her years.

Still, we accept that the things we lose are necessarily lost to make space for the things we gain. We recognize this as a natural, if sometimes difficult, part of development—*except in one stage of life*. When this stage arrives, we are more challenged than at any other time in life to recognize the ebb and flow of loss and gain and to accept the natural symmetry that exists in development.

This stage occurs when both of your parents have died. As a major transitional stage in life, it gets only a nod of recognition. Rarely is it acknowledged as its own independent developmental stage, and even when it is recognized, its incredible power for healing and transformation is underestimated. Seen as a predictable developmental stage of life, becoming parentless loses its sting and instead becomes an opportunity for growth.

Imagine trying to conceive of—or learn from—adolescence if you were to view it as a single, discreet event. Instead, we know it as an unfolding—a time of trying on, discarding, and testing. Or, try to visualize what you could gain, if anything, if you were to see the shift from middle age into old age as one occurrence. Instead, we see aging as a ripening of the body and spirit, an extended process that we hope will bring us to a new level of maturity and wisdom.

Aging includes a time in your life when your parents die. It is at this time that you are orphaned, because you are left without parents. Whether or not you experience the feeling of being an "orphan," you are one, and as an orphan you will mourn for your lost parents; you will mourn for your lost inner child, for your lost childhood. Mourning is never really finished. The same is true of "orphanhood": It may last 5 or 50 years, but it will *not* occur in an afternoon. It is a *process* set in motion at your parents' deaths, but it continues on, creating tidal waves of change. *Your developmental task in this stage is to ride the tidal wave to your potential, rather than allowing it to wash you ashore aimlessly.* It is a time to set goals.

Orphanhood, far from being about death, grief, and living with loss, is ultimately a story about rebirth.

Full Adulthood

Every year 5 percent of the population loses a parent to death. That is a lot of people losing parents and becoming their own authority figures. They are thrown into what I call *full adulthood*. Paradoxically the coming of this stage is also accompanied by an uncomfortable sensitivity or vulnerability:

➤ Feeling little

➤ Feeling like crying

➤ Being overly sensitive

➤ Feeling lost

➤ Being impatient

➤ Feeling anxious

➤ Feeling depressed

➤ Overreacting

➤ Overeating to seek comfort

Who wouldn't admit that facing the feelings that accompany loss brings about a sense of vulnerability? Those who want to grow, heal, and transform, face themselves and their vulnerability head on. That is exactly what *full adulthood* is, and it offers an unparalleled opportunity to do exactly that.

Losing parents creates a change in status unlike any other—and yet it is simultaneously a chance to start anew, one that presents itself at a time when you are most likely to benefit from the opportunity. It can bring about a profound sense of disconnection or aloneness—yet it offers the potential for connection to others in ways that you have never before known, or perhaps even imagined. It may bring up unresolved issues—but it simultaneously brings about the opportunity to reevaluate and let go of many elements of your earlier life experiences—particularly those that were dysfunctional or those that created misery. Parent loss has the potential to take you to the darkest, most closed-off side of human experience as well as to the rich and vibrant opening of your full potential.

The Vulnerability of Loss and Uncertainty

Just as with any other stage of development, the gains of full adulthood are built upon its losses. When you lose someone important in your life, you gain the opportunity to access your most authentic self. When this someone is your parent—and then when it is both parents—the loss is only multiplied because of the significance of the relationship. You lose any remaining claim to your childhood when you lose your parents; when you're not a child, you must grow up with absolute finality. The grief that accompanies this finality sets in motion a chain of events and an emotional process that makes you sensitive. In facing someone's death you may also face your own. However, even if your mortality is not brought to the forefront, as it often isn't for those who lose their parents at an early age, confronting the death of a loved one creates transitions and shifts, calling into question the relationship that existed.

FROM THEN TO NOW

Who Am I Now?	Who Was I Then?	Who Can I Be?
An adult/*A child*	A child	An adult
No one's child/*Someone's child*	Someone's child	No one's child
Free, unfettered/*Caretaker*	Caretaker	Free, unfettered
Responsible to myself/*Responsible to my parents*	Responsible to my parents	Responsible to myself

---

You will find yourself asking many questions when you lose your parents:

> ➤ Does the relationship with my parents still exist?

> ➤ Was it essential to my well-being?

> ➤ Where will I go—to whom—to meet the needs that were met by the person who is now gone?

> ➤ What will I do without the escape to my childhood?

> ➤ Who am I now if I am not someone's child?

> ➤ How did I feel about my mother and father?

> ➤ How did they feel about me?

> ➤ Was our relationship good or bad?

> ➤ What would I change about the relationship?

> ➤ What did I learn from my mother/father?

> ➤ Did they know the *real* me?

> ➤ Did I really know my mother?

> ➤ Did I really know my father?

The transition from being someone's child to losing your parents and being no one's child is a lifelong process. It doesn't occur overnight, and it offers you far more than grief and loss; it offers you the opportunity to choose who you will become.

Transition and Uncertainty

Look at the preceding table and, whether your parents are living or have passed away, fill in the "Who Am I Now?" blocks with several of your present behaviors, roles, and beliefs. The boldface entries represent the types of entries made by someone whose parents are gone;

the italic entries represent entries made by someone whose parents are still living. If your parents are no longer living, go to the "Who Was I Then?" column and consider who you once were and the ways in which you have changed since the death of your parents. If your parents are still living, you'll fill out the table just a bit differently. After filling in the "Who Am I Now?" blocks with several current behaviors, roles, and beliefs, you will fill in the "Who Can I Be?" blocks with who you *believe* you can become and the ways in which you *believe* you may change when you become an orphan.

This exercise illustrates the period of transition that occurs upon the loss of your parents, and it is during this transition that you experience uncertainty. You know who you were, but you do not yet know who you will become. This lack of knowing is what contributes to the sense of vulnerability in orphanhood; you are far more vulnerable when you are uncertain. It is this vulnerability that opens the door to tremendous potential for healing, growth, transformation, and eventually power. It is the power you feel in this stage that ultimately sets you free and allows you a new range of behaviors:

➤ The changed status of your relationship with your parents

➤ Your emotional (and perhaps even physical) well-being after the loss

➤ The realization that you have truly lost connection to your childhood

➤ The sense that you must fully and finally enter adulthood

➤ Your lack of familiarity with how to cope—and cope well—with this loss

Losing your parents is unlike any other loss, and until you have experienced it, you cannot know how to cope with the experience. Once you do survive your loss, you realize it has become time to explore being an adult. What does it mean to you to be an adult? For most, any discussion about adulthood means accepting responsibility; working hard; making plans; thinking things through; establishing lasting relationships; becoming goal oriented; planning for the future.

When your parents die, a window closes but a door opens. It is your choice either to shrink back from the opening or step toward the door, taking in all of the opportunities for sight and sound and movement that await you. The death of your parents starts the story; how it unfolds is up to you. "I never thought about myself as having no parents. It was much too painful. The thought never occurred to me that one day I would reach this stage of life, I never even knew it was a stage," said Barbara, age 61.

As an adult without parents you open your eyes and your heart to another side of the experience, to the gains that can be built upon the losses, to the potential that is created in a vacuum, and to the choices that become available when you are truly free. This is not to suggest that it is unnecessary or even harmful to grieve or mourn; it is decidedly *not*. In fact, the mourning that occurs when you lose your parents is *essential* in order to make room for the growth that you can realize. This is a time rich with opportunities in which the rediscovery of the self is not only possible, but well within your grasp.

Your freedom and your power create an unparalleled opportunity for you to make discoveries about yourself, choose a new or different path for your life, or simply accept the path you have already chosen, but with a consciousness and intent that didn't exist before. Far from dancing on your parents' graves, you are honoring their lives all the more when you follow this opportunity, because you are choosing to take the path toward realizing your full potential.

When you choose this opportunity to rediscover yourself and even create yourself anew, *loss will not be the sole product of losing your parents*. Instead, living without your parents will create the opportunity for rediscovery by making you question who you are and your place in the world. When your parents' voices are silenced, you may experience a profound sense of aloneness and subsequently begin to experience a loss of love and authority in your life. Yet the potential is there to experience a powerful awareness of your connection to others. The potential is there for you to experience your own love, your own specific power, and your own unique authority.

All of these components of this developmental stage combine and press upon you, forming a need to rediscover yourself—and that rediscovery is the plot of *your new* story. This crisis and its power to transform you is what we'll explore next as we move toward the dénouement: understanding *how* you can transform deep loss into abundant gain, unbounded grief into unbridled joy, and untapped potential into breathtaking reality.

A Crisis of Identity: Who Am I?

Michael, age 53, had tremendous amounts of musical ability that he expressed throughout his life. He was a pianist. Yet, at home he was rarely asked to play for his parents. At the very same time he heard clear messages about going to college and becoming a professional, as in dentist or doctor, like all the other men in the family. He was depressed during many periods of his life. He had put away his musical proclivity for good and it took a toll on him. In fact, it took years to convince him that he would be happier and more complete if he renewed his creative ability. It wasn't until his father died, when Michael was in his fifties, that he slowly returned to the piano. Even that began as a fluke. He had suggested to his daughter that she purchase a piano for her home and, one year, visiting her at Thanksgiving, he sat down and began to play. When he returned to therapy the next week, he was filled with rage. "Why wasn't I encouraged to follow my gift?" he demanded. "Everyone knew I could play piano well! Why wasn't I encouraged by my parents?"

Power: The Silencing of the Parental Voice

The loss of a parent brings about uncertainty that results in vulnerability. This vulnerability in turn creates an increased need for resolution in your life. You will not remain in the painful state of uncertainty and vulnerability forever, and your sense of inner power will eventually emerge.

When you lose your parents you are losing two of the most significant anchors in your life; if nothing else, you were always someone's child. Suddenly you find yourself faced with an essential question: *Who am I now?* Your thoughts and beliefs about who you are—your self-concept, in other words—is inextricably bound to the internalized lessons you learned from your parents: the attitudes, values, and behaviors they instilled in you. Your voice developed out of the voice that belonged to your parents, just as their voices grew from their experiences with their own parents, and so on through the generations. In fact, the voices of your parents are so important in your development that they become your own in many ways, although we are often unconscious of the *extent* to which we echo their teachings.

When your parents are alive, they provide the foundation that tells you who you are, that you matter, and that childhood is always just a memory away. No matter how much your conscious self embraces adulthood, it is reassuring to feel the safety net of childhood resting beneath you. Part of the uncertainty of losing your parents is about this very fact. Regardless of the reality—whether you have a spouse, children, or friends who seem on the surface to meet this same requirement or, for that matter, whether warmth or indifference marks your relationship with your parents—your parents are the ones who first made a place for you in the world. They brought you to life; they noticed what happened to you; they were connected to you in ways no one else could ever be. Common sentiments expressed by respondents were, "Who else will ever worry about me like that?" "Who will care about me like they did?" "Who can I turn to if I need something? I no longer have a safety net." Your parents created you—and they occupy a powerful and uncontested place in your life.

Many people look outside of themselves for the sounds that will fill the silence created when their parents pass away. They keep busy; they begin new relationships or focus on old ones; they distract themselves by replacing the quiet with noise of any sort—so long as they can avoid the pain left by the fact that their parents are gone.

You must listen to the silence in order to mourn—and you must mourn in order to heal and transform. It is through listening that you recognize that a silence exists, and it is through recognizing the silence that you feel the full range of emotions associated with your loss. This includes the early, tentative feelings that accompany healing and transformation: hope, possibility, and an unfamiliar sense of freedom. One of the first and most significant feelings, however, will be that of profound aloneness, and although remaining open to this aloneness can be difficult and painful, it is essential. You must first fully occupy the space left by the loss of your parents in order to take tenancy of your own life as you want it to be.

Aloneness: The Absence of Love and Authority

In the void left by your parents' deaths you will begin to hear the sound of your own voice forming. Many people might argue that what your voice first tells you will not be easy to hear. Although the message carried through the silence—that you are alone—can carry fear and sorrow, it is also a message of hope. The very realization of your aloneness creates the need for rediscovery. In the space of your identity crisis and the vacuum created by the silencing of your parents' voices, you will hear the call to rediscover who you are. It is only then that you will begin to form the desire to create a new identity.

Colin Murray Parkes calls this period of bereavement—the time in which you form a new identity—a "psychosocial transition."[1] This transition is marked by the deprivation caused by the absence of those people who provided the essential "supplies" of life. These supplies, the love and authority extended to you by your parents, were the psychological equivalents of food and drink. Even when you were unconscious of their place in your life, they were necessary to your survival. Their absence in your life leaves a substantial and noticeable gap. Their absence also increases the feelings of uncertainty and the questions about how—and even whether—you can cope.

While the death of parents obviously produces a sense of loss, I am emphasizing *gain*: transition, growth, and opportunity. This is what can occur in the absence or gap created by your parents' deaths. Parkes acknowledges the duality of loss and this potential gain, noting that "Every change involve[s] both a loss and a gain."[2]

Even though you are likely to be an adult when your parents die, you still feel the absence of their love and authority, the secure boundaries they created for you, and the family traditions that you associate with them. The absence of all of these things cannot help but create a vacuum, and it is in this vacuum that you experience a sort of existential aloneness that outruns the fleeting feelings of aloneness that we all experience from time to time. At the same time that you are experiencing the sadness and loneliness associated with this loss, you can begin to enjoy the freedom that comes from the absence of the restraint that your parents represented in your life. Finding this freedom, however, takes time. This search for yourself and for the joy that accompanies rediscovering yourself is what occupies the space in time between your loss and your gain. In the transition, however, you will also experience profound discomfort. Know, though, that this discomfort is essential to finding your new place in the world.

As Cynthia, age 51, described her feelings about losing her parents, she cried desperately, like a brokenhearted child. Over our next several sessions, as Cynthia began to explore the realization that there was no escape from her sorrow—*and that the only relief was that which she could offer herself*—she experienced a profound and paradoxical sense of healing. She would no longer be waiting for someone else to make things better. In the most final way, she was no longer a child, and that gave her a freedom she'd never had.

During her therapy, Cynthia described the loss of her parents as the single most uncomfortable experience she'd ever had: "I was independent and had a family and close friends, yet was terrified by not having my parents. I felt as if no one cared about me anymore. I had lost the two people who really cared if I lived or died when push came to shove, and I felt truly abandoned because of it."

Cynthia's comments and experience illustrate the reality that part of the bereavement process is about learning to live without the physical connection to your parents and the built-in comfort they provided—and this is true even if the comfort is untapped. As your childhood falls away, you will know the intense emotional, and even spiritual, experience of losing the parental structure of love and authority. Indeed, you *have* lost the security and safety of your family in a very real way.

WHEN GRIEF IS INTRACTABLE

The table below illustrates Elisabeth Kubler-Ross's five stages of grief. These stages have long been accepted by experts in death and dying, medical care, and mental health. The stages and symptoms listed here are to be expected when a loved one dies, with the symptoms having a proportional relationship to the closeness and interdependence of the relations.[3] It is the degree of the symptoms that indicates whether you are stuck in grief or progressing through it normally and productively. Although there are no absolutes in terms of timelines or symptoms, when grieving interferes with going about the daily activities of living after more than a few weeks, it is wise to seek counsel from a mental health professional.

The Kubler-Ross Stages of Grieving

STAGE OF GRIEVING	SIGNS AND SYMPTOMS OF EACH STAGE
Denial	Refusal to accept the death, unwillingness to discuss/acknowledge it
Resentment	Why me? Blame of God, doctors, others who are healthy
Bargaining	Promises to change behaviors/beliefs if the loved one is spared
Depression	Sorrow over the death or impending death; joy absent from life
Acceptance	Calmly accepting/facing death, seeing life stages in perspective

It is precisely *because* of the discomfort created by the unfamiliar difficult feelings that you desire change. If you listen carefully, you can see your own desire for change and the seeds of the changes themselves carried on a wind of freedom that comes through the silence.

The voice may whisper at first—or it may sing—but the words are the same:

> ➤ The needs or goals of your parents no longer hold you.

> ➤ This is the time for you to begin anew.

> ➤ You are fully in charge of your life from this point forward.

> ➤ What are you going to do with this opportunity?

When your parents die, it can activate the awareness that you, too, are going to die. For those who are younger when they become orphans, this is not necessarily a part of the experience. However, those past middle age are likely to face their own mortality upon the death of their parents, and this is yet another push toward rediscovery.

Whether your desire for rediscovery has its roots in the discomfort that the feelings of orphanhood bring about or in the growing awareness of your own mortality—or both—the bottom line is the same: *Inaction is not an option*. The chief task of this developmental stage of adulthood is to act—and to act now—to rediscover yourself. Recognizing that you have new freedoms and becoming aware that time is limited and life is finite fortify the desire to realize your potential and reach out for your dreams.

A Change in Status

Grasping the meaning of having no parents and the crisis it generates is the first step toward rewriting your story when you lose your parents. The second step involves your change in status. This change first involves a growing *awareness* of both the concrete and less tangible shifts that result at this stage of life. Following that growing awareness is *acceptance* of these changes. Awareness and acceptance run as parallel paths on the same journey, and there are no shortcuts. You must take the road that exists, no matter its length. It is only when you have traversed these paths that you can move forward toward a transformation in which you learn to live without your parents and to let go of unresolved issues.

Next in Line

At some point you have recognized that you are mortal, but denial of mortality is very common. When your parents die, you have to deal with two aspects of death: their present death and your eventual death. Accepting the notion of your own death is contrary to your own life instinct. As difficult as it may seem, the awareness of mortality is going to surface. It creates a dilemma that you are going to resolve by committing to live your life fully every day. You put the awareness of your mortality in the background. It is not repressed, it is just not in focus.

Mark lost his mother the year he turned 40, and although her death was unexpected and painful, he carried on with his life and didn't get stuck in a mourning phase. Less than a year later, when his father died, he found himself in a very different position: "It was an awareness I felt all over my body, one I could absolutely not ignore. I *got* it. I was going to die—not tomorrow maybe, but I wasn't getting away with escaping it."

Until Mark lost both parents and became an orphan, he kept the awareness of his own mortality at bay, an experience common to many people. Although he had watched his mother die and certainly knew on a vague intellectual level that he too would die someday, he kept the awareness locked safely away in his head, unacknowledged—and far, far away from his heart. It wasn't until his father's death left him without the layer of protection that "childhood" offers—however old the child—that deep, genuine awareness truly hit home for Mark.

Celia, age 47, had discussed death with her parents in a frank and open manner. Yet when her mother died nine years after her father and Celia became an orphan, she realized that she'd held onto an image of parent loss that didn't fit at all with her new experiences: "I grieved deeply, but what struck me was that I wasn't suddenly pitiful. I wasn't as alone or terrified as I'd always just assumed I would be. We were very close, and so I'd always thought that losing my parents would destroy me."

Celia had no idea what it meant to be an orphan at her stage of life. As far as she was concerned, orphans were only children. You simply cannot recognize yourself as an orphan because orphans are abandoned, sad "Oliver Twists" who are truly alone in the world. This image is burned deep into our collective psyche. When you carry this image around, however unwittingly, seeing yourself as an orphan also means seeing yourself as helpless, hopeless, and abandoned.

It is not necessary to allow this perception to serve as your model; it is outdated and unproductive. Instead, you can redefine and rewrite orphanhood—as we are doing here—so that it is empowering and rich with potential. Nonetheless, if this *is* your model of orphanhood and orphans, even if it is buried deep in your consciousness, it is yet another explanation for the difficulty in coming to an awareness of yourself as an orphan. By understanding and overcoming these obstacles to becoming aware of your status as an orphan, you take the first essential step toward the acceptance that is so necessary for transformation and growth.

Acceptance of Changed Status

The rich potential for self-discovery is something you can include in your life. Accepting yourself now may seem like a simple concept, yet for many it is extremely difficult. Whatever reasons resonate with you, however, what is most essential is that you accept your changed status as an adult if you are to become aware of and be able to access your changed identity.

A primary reason for the difficulty we have in accepting ourselves in loss is also a practical reason: the absence of someone you love can create upheaval, havoc, and daily distress in your life. Perhaps you relied heavily upon your parents and saw them or spoke to them frequently. Perhaps their presence was a part of your everyday life. Recognize that accepting parent loss means accepting changes at the very core of your life. This can be incredibly painful, and therefore something to avoid.

Some people deny the impact of parent loss because of the *weak* attachment they had with one or both parents. If you never felt bonded with your parents—always feeling somewhat like an orphan to begin with, in fact—it can be difficult to accept the reality that any chance at a childhood is now lost. It is hard to know how to leave behind something you never had.

Leslie, age 44, often talked about the tough childhood she had. Her father had been in prison off and on for years and her mother had rarely been available—she was always exhausted from working, trying to hold the family together. When Leslie's father died, in fact, Leslie had long since lost touch with him. His death just didn't affect her because he seemed like a stranger. She found it far more difficult—and it took far longer—to accept the loss of her mother, in large part because it brought into focus so many painful gaps in Leslie's childhood: "By the time I was a teenager I believed I'd given up any hope of having a real mother. When I was a kid she was too busy to pay attention and by the time she was available it just felt like prying to me. Now, I regret the past. There was so much water under the bridge by the time I grew up that I didn't try to have a real relationship with her, and I wish I had. I saw her a few times a year on holidays, but it was like seeing some distant cousin. When she died it took me over a year to even admit to myself that I was grieving, but one day, I began to realize that she was the only mother I was ever going to get. I started replaying little things, wishing I'd said something different or been nicer or thanked her for how hard she worked to keep us safe. It was too late by then, and all I have left of her and me is regret."

As Leslie's regret illustrates, a failure to accept the death of your parents, which is tantamount to a failure to accept your new status as an adult, stalls you in your mourning. The grief doesn't go away; it merely stays hidden, lying in wait for your awareness and acceptance. When your new role breaks through your consciousness and then ultimately shifts into a sense of acceptance, a light comes on and illuminates everything inside you and everything around you.

You can't truly know what your new life is about until you begin to explore it. For too many people, unfortunately, life is spent in the dark that is created when they reject awareness and refuse to accept life as it is, unpleasantness and pain included. They waste energy and time resisting reality as if resisting it will *change* reality simply because they refuse to know and accept that life is messy. This resistance can continue to play out during orphanhood. When this happens, there is a deeper loss that is added to the loss of your parents; the time you have wasted can never be regained and the lessons remain unlearned.

Direct your energy toward discovering that you are rich with the potential of a life peopled by "selves" waiting to be recognized and brought to life. These selves can be discovered and honored in the space that is created when your parents die—many of them, in fact, could not emerge from the shadows until now. But in order for this to happen you must do two things. In letting go of the past: You must learn to live without the contact that existed with your parents, and you must let go of unresolved issues.

In addition, for some there is less of a feeling of loss than might be expected. These people feel their parents around them all the time. They feel the presence of their parents. They feel the connection and the memory of their parents remain strong. They are comforted by these feelings and report not feeling orphaned at all.

Letting Go of the Past

As soon as we can form thoughts, we form conscious wishes. This is part of what makes us unique among animals. Although a less enlightened animal wishes for food or shelter, we have not only the consciousness to be *aware* of our desires, but also the complexity to build and direct a life layered upon them.

As you grow, you build a fire that burns bright with dreams and hopes and plans and goals; some you hold onto, pursue, and realize; others whisper themselves off like ashes into the wind. Looking into the fire to find the sparks it once held—sparks that didn't catch in part because of your relationship with your parents—is a piece of the task that awaits you now. This task can be challenging and can even feel traitorous at times, as if you are blaming your parents for any failure you've experienced or any way in which your potential hasn't been realized. However, blame is not the point. Far from shrugging your disappointments, misfires, or dashed hopes off onto your parents, you are exploring the ways in which the bond—strong or weak, good or bad—influenced you in the choices you made, and, most importantly, *continue to do so*. This chapter in your story has two imperatives: first, you need to learn to live without your parents, but *with* yourself; and second, you must identify and let go of your unresolved issues with your parents.

Learning to Live without Your Parents

We have already briefly discussed the need to learn to live without the presence of your parents in your life, but I want to emphasize that this need is a practical challenge as well as an emotional one. Learning this lesson results in a different experience for everyone because relationships between parents and their children differ in so many ways—even two children of the same parents have very different relationships with their parents.

It is hard to imagine, before you lost your parents, how the loss will present itself in your life; there are so many moments, both conscious and unconscious, that are influenced by the relationship you had. If you were close to your parents and involved frequently in their lives, even on a daily basis perhaps, the loss will show up in the small moments and events of everyday life as well. The roles you played will figure in heavily. If your parents have been your rescuers, saving you from everything from flat tires to yourself, the loss will open a door to independence and competence if you allow it to. If you had a less needy relationship, the loss will make itself known differently. You'll experience it on holidays, perhaps, or on Saturday mornings when you had your once-a-week phone call. Whatever your experience, though, the central challenge of your new life is to reweave the fibers of your life wherever they unravel when your parents are no longer part of the daily or weekly fabric.

The reweaving you must do can only be done over time. As much as you might wish to hurry through mourning you cannot. You cannot hurry it up without giving up the opportunity—the gains. I believe that this is the true meaning and instruction behind the saying that time heals all wounds. In the space following the death of your parents, you lose much. But you gain, too. You gain the time to heal, to experience new feelings, and to rediscover yourself. This healing cannot occur without loving support from within yourself—and from those around you.

Unresolved Issues with Parent(s)

The healing that must occur for transformation to take place can only be done completely and successfully if you are truthful with yourself about the relationship that existed—its strengths and its weaknesses, its grace and its flaws. Whatever remains unresolved is an unrepaired tear in the fabric, and these tears, whether there are 2 or 20, weaken the weave throughout the entire cloth. Eventually the tears spread, the fabric rends easily, and the damage extends not only into your past, but into your future as well.

It is essential that you do the work of closing out unresolved issues and healing old wounds. As we continue rewriting the story of parent loss, we will touch upon this issue a number of times in different ways, because it is critically important. Learning how to let go of closely held feelings about past events as you learn how to avoid replaying them in your present and future relationships is paramount to the success of those relationships.

Exploring Your Potential

Throughout your new life without your parents, you are going to find out things about yourself that allow you to develop the potential that has been undeveloped, hidden, or even unknown in the shadows of the relationship you had with your parents. Just as your parents influenced who you became by their very existence, in your life without your parents you have the freedom to *re*-create yourself. This is the challenge—and the reward—of parent loss. You are starting on a new journey, rewriting the story of who you are and who you choose to be.

When you lose your parents, *your life can truly become **about you**, for the first time.* How you will change is an open question; the sky is the limit. The way you change can suddenly be in direct relationship with your needs, without any of the kind of self-censorship that may have been the natural outgrowth of the influence your parents had on your life. You will likely benefit the most from rediscovering and connecting with what you have suppressed. This is not to say that your parents inhibited you purposely, kept you clinging to an old outdated image of yourself, or intentionally forced you to be someone or something that is really not you. The truth is more subtle and has more texture than that. Your desire to please your parents was combined with your own likes and dislikes, which were in large part formed under the influence of your parents' values, tastes, fears, and dreams. Without casting blame, parts of the real you got lost in the translation.

Now you are free to rediscover, or maybe to discover for the first time, who you truly want to be in the world. You are the one who decides what is important to change and what is not. You will have the exciting opportunity to make these decisions on your own. You do not need to follow anyone else's path or fulfill anyone else's needs, only your own; and your challenge now is to use this new awareness to find your own way so you can fulfill your own potential.

2

The Quality of
Parental Relationships

Be it life or death, we crave only reality.

—*Henry David Thoreau*, Walden

Becoming the person you were meant to be is a lifetime process and the injunction to "be yourself" echoes in your head like a familiar soundtrack. You know who you are; you know what you want; you know the tune your inner voice plays. Your inner voice beckons to you through intuition and this voice, your voice, indicates that there just may be a plan for you. How clearly you hear your voice and whether or not you listen to it determines how self aware and responsive you are and have been to your inner core speaking to you through this voice.

Your unique nature will, hopefully, naturally emerge. Your adolescence and young adulthood were filled with dreams and intentions: There were times in life when obvious choices were made and decisions about your life's purpose required answers. What am I going to do with myself? Who will I become? These are typical early life examinations and are considered normal, natural, and predictable.

What was not predicted is how you would feel when your parents died. This is a question you never asked yourself. Who does? After the death of your parents, when the status of being no one's child ushers in the feelings of vulnerability, aloneness, pain, and fear, you may be overwhelmed.

You are the parent now, whether or not you have your own children, because you have become your own parent. You have become an *adult*. This is a time of life when you ask the same questions you asked yourself in adolescence or young adulthood. What will I be now? The most honest news about this transition in your life is this: *The loss of parents can be an exhilarating opportunity for you. Limitless possibilities await.*

Remember, it is possible to accept the process of mourning; become aware of self; allow the consciousness and intention of change; watch yourself carefully for cues to what you want to do and who you are becoming. This will be different for everyone whether you are 25, 35, or 45 years old; male or female; married or single; part of a small or large family; rich or poor.

How Close Were You to Your Parents? Did Your Closeness Hinder Your Independence?

Losing parents is a life crisis that requires management. The familiar and comfortable parental relationships you have come to depend upon for support or motivation are gone. How do you cope with the loss of a parent you loved? Do not be naïve. Losing your parents and becoming no one's child is a psychic shock. Whether or not you relate to being orphaned, you have sustained a major life blow. Therefore, you will be stressed. What are the steps you must go through? What do you do about unfinished business between you and a parent who has died? Are these steps different if you were close to your parents rather than if you were not?

Resolving issues with people you have lost may not seem possible, but it is possible. Much of the actual work is accomplished through the conscious process of mourning. This requires thinking, bringing up memories, writing letters or keeping journals, making lists of the things that are necessary to address. Those who mourn "well" grieve for days about the lost parent, allowing themselves to feel all the emotions that rise to the surface. There will be many—from anger to despair to sadness to pain.

You may find it helpful to have an inner dialogue with your deceased parent. An *inner dialogue* is talking to your parent as though he or she were still alive. First, either silently or out loud, you start the conversation. Then you imagine what your parent would say back to you, and so on. You may find this a useful exercise in order to clear the air and express unresolved feelings. This dialogue may actually become a conversation that occurs at the grave of your parent. Many visit their parents' graves to work through their feelings about them and discuss issues. Sarah, age 43, said, "I felt like I heard my mother's voice in my head and she was saying really nice things to me." Barry, age 54, commented, "For the first time I actually opened up to Dad, as he lay there in the ground. . . . Did I need that safety net for me to be so vulnerable?"

How did you cope with the loss of your parents? Did you:

➤ Cry?

➤ Scream?

➤ Become depressed?

➤ Go numb?

➤ Hide your feelings?

➤ Pretend the situation was less painful than it actually was?

➤ Cope with the grief alone?

➤ Share it with others?

➤ Talk to your therapist, your best friend, your spouse?

➤ Become remote and withdraw socially?

➤ Act out and give yourself permission to "do anything you wanted?"

➤ Develop physical symptoms?

How long did your grief last? How long before you stopped picking up the phone to call your parent? How long did you wish your parent would suddenly appear and tell you it was all a bad dream? Or were you consumed with so much negative feeling that you found yourself drowning in guilt or remorse.

Stephanie, age 56, is an example of someone who was so close to her mom that when her mother died, Stephanie had a very difficult time returning to a normal life. She mourned for two years and felt socially withdrawn and depressed. She felt no happiness at all. Without her mother, whom she described as her best friend, she felt unable to cope with life and had little zest for living. Her inner child was in turmoil, and Stephanie could not seem to adjust to being the "adult I know I should be. . . . If I could just feel better I would be okay."

Stephanie had done her grieving, but she was not moving forward. Why? She was stuck in the position of wishing her mother would return, waiting for someone else to take care of her dependency needs, and resisting making the *choice* to grow up and take full responsibility for her own life.

Maryanne, age 48, another woman who was very close to her mother, had an experience very similar to Stephanie's. Her dependency on her mother had been so great that when her mother died, Maryanne was so overwhelmed with the cycling of strong emotions she was practically immobilized for months. She stopped exercising and taking care of herself. She cried all the time, became irritable with her husband and children, and blamed her sister for not taking good enough care of their mother.

Maryanne had a very tough time with this death. She soon realized that under the emotional turmoil were very angry feelings toward her mother over certain aspects of their relationship. When she finally became conscious of them and ultimately realized she needed to establish a stronger sense of her mature, productive, and effective side, she was able to recognize that she had "a lot of psychological work to do on myself, and I hope I can do it. Only then will I feel better."

Adaptation Allows Progress to Continue

Accepting the deaths of your parents is the first step you have to take to come to terms with your own need to grow again. Yet *acceptance* is not a reliable term. Over the years there has been a movement to use the term *adaptation* to death instead of acceptance. Adaptation is kinder, and perhaps more realistic.

When my last parent died, leaving me alone, I was stunned by the explosion of feelings and emotions that emerged. My own personal experience was what originally motivated me to write this book. When I examined the lives of my patients and friends who shared this stage of life called "adult orphanhood," I noticed similar reactions, and it became clear that orphanhood was a stage unto itself.

Having no parents is a stage highlighted by:

➤ Loss of elders

➤ Loss of authority figures

➤ Shift from vulnerability to a sense of your own power

➤ You assume authority

➤ You express power through your own unique voice

➤ Your unique voice reconnects to your deepest self

Having no parents is a stage with its own fertility: the ability to create in a most gratifying and unbelievable way. What is important to know is that you can change, and you can change in limitless ways. Change is *integral to grief and loss*.

You have a new role. You are now in full adulthood, in full maturity, in a position of power and authority and head of the family.

What If You Were Close?

Individuals I have treated or interviewed over the years have experienced their relationships with their parents in different ways. Feelings of closeness to parents varied from individual to individual. For the most part, the kinds of relationships people have with their parents fall into the following categories: very close, moderately close, distant, angry, and detached.

Generally, the closer the relationship you enjoyed with your parents, the greater the sense of loss you felt at the time of their deaths.

Therefore, the more you have loved, the more you have to lose. It is terribly painful to sustain the loss of someone close to you. In the book *Loss and Bereavement: Managing Change,* Ros Weston says, "Loss is painful and the bigger the loss the bigger the pain. Because the loss is painful, the intensity of the pain we suffer from the loss of someone so close to us can make us go to great lengths to minimize the pain, or to avoid it entirely. Whether such tactics are in the long run helpful, healthy, or unavoidable remains to be seen."[1]

The loss of a parent releases feelings, thoughts, images, and memories that seem to come in waves, which are triggered by almost anything. For example, a patient in his mid-fifties reported that during an ordinary visit to the gym he was overwhelmed with feelings of despair while in the sauna. He remembered having been taken to a steam bath when he was 7 years old by his father, who had recently passed away. He was flooded with thoughts about what his father's life had been like.

Despite the unpleasant nature of his experience, it was a positive indication that his grieving was normal. Even though he felt badly, it was important for him to acknowledge his grief and to consciously manage his feelings instead of finding ways to avoid them.

Managing grief means:

➤ Allowing yourself to feel your feelings

➤ Staying open no matter what

➤ Finding support systems

➤ Sharing your feelings with another

➤ Realizing the natural cycles within grief

What If You Were Not Close?

For those of you who were not close to your parents, your loss may involve other feelings as well. For those of you left with angry relationships, there may be feelings of guilt that you can choose either to resolve or to live with. You may have found that what you might have given up in closeness with your parents years ago was replaced with whatever enriched your life—like making your own decisions and choices without regard for your "elders."

Sue, age 49, is a professional woman who admitted that she would have liked to have been closer to her mother. When her father died early in Sue's life, she felt devastated. It was obvious to Sue that her relationship with her father would have been more important to her if he had lived longer. Without closeness to her mother, Sue describes how she always did whatever she wanted to do whenever she wanted to do it. "I didn't really think about how my actions would affect my mom; after age 17 I became extremely independent."

Brad, age 50, is a businessman who reported no change in his life whatsoever since the death of his parents, except that he no longer had to visit them. He was fairly resistant to any discussion regarding his psychological or emotional status and didn't really connect to being an orphan. This is a common response from some people, more often for males than for females.

If you were not close but want the benefits of parent loss:

➤ Begin to explore your parental relationships from wherever you are now.

➤ Release any negative feelings and put them in the past.

➤ Imagine yourself in a state of re-creation.

➤ Find something about your life that you want to begin.

Factors That Affect Your Degree of Loss

Many factors that have nothing to do with intimacy or conflict affect how the loss of parents will touch your life. Your age, your marital status, the place you are in your life's development, how involved your parents were in your adult life, your place in the family, whether or not you had siblings, your role as caregiver during illness, and your gender are some factors.

Which parent you lose is also significant. Generally, it appears to be more difficult to lose a mother, although a father's death often matters as much to men. The death of a mother may be harder to adjust to than the death of a father, according to Jane Littlewood. In her book, *Aspects of Grief and Bereavement in Adult Life*, she says, "The mother's role as a nurturing caretaker continues with respect to her children into their adult life."[2] Your mother is generally the first person you call other than your spouse when you are in trouble. That's how much people still rely on Mom's nurturing, even into adulthood. Yet for some, calling mother would be the last thing they would want to do.

I can remember a conversation with a lovely 70-year-old man with sparkling blue eyes and white silvery hair, who sat on a Board of Directors with me a few years ago. He knew I was writing this book and would occasionally contribute an idea of his from his own experience. He had recently lost his own mother. One day after a meeting, this man took my hand and said, "Dr. Butler, listen to this. My very own mother has been gone for over a year. I still hear her voice and I still want to reach out to speak to her. Every night before I went to bed, I used to call her, just to check in and see how she was feeling. I was her only son. Now, even though she has been gone for a year, I still reach for the phone to call her in the evenings. Just think of it. I am an old man myself and I still act like a good boy. I will always miss my mother."

The mystery of motherhood pulls at your heartstrings forever. To think we may always need contact with the mother who nurtured us can be both wonderful and scary. "My mother was always there for me no matter what. How can I ever replace that? It is a fact of life that hurts a lot," said Paula, age 34.

Maxine Harris writes in *The Loss That Is Forever*, "For most, the loss of a parent registers as a ten on an emotional Richter scale. The solid ground beneath one's feet no longer exists, and that which held things together and made them solid and secure is gone."[3] She then quotes C. S. Lewis, whose own mother died when he was nine: "With my mother's death all settled happiness, all that was tranquil and reliable, disappeared from my life. There was to be much fun, many pleasures, many stabs at Joy; but no more of the old security. It was sea and islands now; the great continent had sunk like Atlantis."

"Solid ground was forever gone from Lewis's life, and while he could experience moments when he felt secure and stable, often he felt as if he were being tossed about in an unsteady sea."[4]

In one case, Carly, age 50, despite many problems with both of her parents, found her way to self-acceptance and peace with them:

No one had more difficulty with her parents than I. Both of my parents were really difficult. My dad was in the clothing business and my mother worked for him. They were always traveling for business, leaving my brother and me alone with our grandparents. It felt like they were so infrequently home. My brother and I got very little in the way of attention, recognition, or reinforcement for the things we did well. Thank goodness for our grandparents. If it hadn't been for them I don't know where my brother and I would have ended up!

Yet, as I matured, I realized that they were both such hard workers they really weren't the kind of people who should have had children. I was angry for years and acted out in many ways. For example, I did poorly in school. I ran away once to my girlfriend's house. I had inappropriate boy friends and barely made it to college. Fortunately, I became attracted to a strong guy with a good solid family, and I married early to get away from my own distant and unavailable parents.

My father died suddenly of a heart attack when I was in my early forties, and my mother took over the business. Although she actively grieved, she never changed her ways. Mom still remained emotionally cool and numbed her feelings with ideas of taking Dad's business international. Five years later, Mom was diagnosed with liver cancer and she was dead within a year. I couldn't believe life could be so cruel. Both of my parents dead within six years!

But I must have been born under a lucky star because between Dad's death and her diagnosis, I had begun therapy with my husband. As a result, my therapist encouraged me to deal with my feelings of anger toward my mother. At first, I was so terribly resistant to the idea, but then it occurred to me that it made sense to deal with my bad feelings before she died, so I could be there for her if she were ever to get sick, without always trying to prove to her what a rotten mother she had been.

My plan turned out for the best. As a result of my work, when my mother did die, I was left with very little to think about. Of course, there is never a good time for someone's mother to die, and I certainly could have said I love you one more time, but basically, I was left with few regrets. I had made my amends. I had crossed the bridge. She had died being friends with her daughter, and I was proud of my attempts to fix things before it all happened.

Although experiencing the loss of a loved person is always traumatic, it may be difficult for different reasons at all stages of life. The significance of close relationships increases during middle age, perhaps because our values change or perhaps because our proximity to death increases. We come to value more highly those people in our lives to whom we are attached. Their loss feels worse and has greater existential meaning during this time. "To lose something or somebody is to be deprived of and separated from a presence around which or with whom we have organized our lives, and it represents a challenge to our assumptive world."[5] Separation from those who helped us to develop the framework of our lives creates a significant absence that causes us to confront the basis of our worldview.

Losing parents, whether in your childhood or in your twenties, certainly can be overwhelming—but for entirely different reasons. At an early age you are losing the potential of having those parents around for role identification and financial or emotional support. They might have given direction for your developing life, but their relationship has not been laden with the specificity that grows from many years of influence. Factors that affect the experience of loss as an adult are the following:

➤ The degree of closeness experienced between parent and adult

➤ Time spent as an adult with the parent

➤ How much energy and activity had been shared with the parent as an adult

➤ The role the parent still plays in the life of the adult

Frozen Grief

Those who have antipathetic or destructive relationships with their parents often grieve with an intense aspect of guilt, remorse, regret, or denial. Or, they don't grieve at all. This is unfortunate because their orphanhood is then consumed with the effort to resolve negative feelings or experiences. Their efforts can absorb a great deal of time and energy and may last for months or even years and may result in a condition known as "frozen grief." Frozen grief can be released by choosing to become aware of the feelings of grief.

Anthony, age 45, is a businessman who described his relationship with his mother as "fair," while describing his relationship with his recently deceased father as bad. Anthony insisted that being orphaned just meant less for him to do: no more middle-of-the-night hospital visits, no more grocery shopping and making sure the caregiver had what was necessary for "Dad's needs." Anthony was not the primary caregiver. His younger brother and someone they hired assumed most of the burden.

As usual, Anthony felt little love or connection to what he described as a cold and critical father. His grieving consisted of remembering all the hurts his father had caused him, and he eased his negative emotions through the use of alcohol. When his drinking finally enraged his wife, she literally dragged him into therapy.

Carl, also age 40, felt a similar parental detachment from his father upon his death and also described feeling guilty about never having been able to mend the broken relationship. His feelings of remorse and guilt were so severe, Carl became severely moody and depressed.

Carl attempted to cope with the onslaught of emotion through denial, channeling his emotional life into playing golf until he was exhausted. Even though he played several times a week, his efforts to contain his emotions were less than effective. One day in marital counseling his wife divulged the truth about Carl by saying, "We all know what is really going on with Carl. He is running away from looking at how he feels now that his father is gone. His father was a big part of his life and he chooses just not to talk about it."

"I Was Always Myself"

There are always those lucky adults who feel their identities were not threatened by parental boundaries. These people feel good about themselves, have positive self esteem, feel they made their own choices in life, did the things they wanted to do, and were happy, secure, and actualized folks.

Michele, a successful college professor in her fifties, was one of these individuals and described her relationship with her parents, who have now both died, as moderately connected. She said all the children in the family were encouraged to excel in academics but were also encouraged to explore themselves as individuals. Although the message they received in their house pointed them toward becoming "professionals," she felt that if any of the kids had wanted to do something different, they probably could have. They were encouraged to "become themselves." In Michele's family, structure and discipline were important factors. The children knew clearly what was expected of them, and they all had responsibilities in the house. The fact that they all turned out well and did become professionals is, in her terms, "the benefit of good fortune."

When I asked Michele if she felt orphaned, she said, "Yes, I guess I am an orphan, but I don't dwell on it. I am just living the rest of my own life now. But, I sure do miss my parents." When asked if she had unresolved issues, she said, "No." When asked if she intended to make changes in her life, she said, "Probably not."

Interestingly, Michele had a younger sister named Marta. Marta was the youngest in the family and had always been slightly babied.

She described herself as a good girl who did what was expected. She was an artistic type who, although she studied and became an art therapist, always wanted to be flamboyant and bohemian. When her parents died, the effect on Marta was predictably more dramatic.

She left her "safe" job as an art therapist in a hospital and took a big risk, doing something she had always wanted to do. She began taking sculpting classes and reinvented herself as an artist. She describes herself as happy and says, "I have really changed, and everything that has happened to me feels good and for the best."

Strong personalities that are more prone to self-actualization seem to adapt more easily to the drive for growth and transformation provided by orphanhood. In an article entitled "The Role of Hardiness in the Resolution of Grief," Jane Campbell, Paul Swank, and Ken Vincent suggest, "The resolution of grief . . . is related to personality traits such as hardiness. . . . Hardy people are described as committed to their activities, feeling they have a sense of control over their lives, and seeing life as a series of challenges."[6]

Therefore, being "hardy" is the best predictor for enjoying the advantages of managing grief well and exploring your new adult life to the fullest. To have a hardy approach, it is necessary to do the following:

1. Commit to your grief process.

2. See the grief process as a challenge and accept all feelings and thoughts as important.

3. Accept the challenge of self-discovery by constantly believing in yourself and your right to be fully happy and joyful.

How to Resolve Issues in the Absence of Parents

I recommend keeping a journal as you read this book. There will be many opportunities for you to keep track of your feelings, thoughts, and impressions.

In your journal, answer the following questions:

1. Identify your goal, is it to get over anger? Remove a psychological barrier to intimacy from something that occurred from parenting? Other?

2. Work it through by means of inner dialogue, discussion with deceased parent, imagined communications, talking directly to parent at graveside, written letter.

3. Share this information with a therapist, spouse, friend, or sibling.

How to Resolve Issues before Parents Die

This exercise is good for anyone who has lost a parent. In your exercise journal, write down the following questions and answer them for yourself. Write a few more sentences describing your response.

1. How would I describe my relationship with my mother? My father?

2. What was good/bad about these relationships?

3. What was the nature of the conflict with my mother/my father?

4. Am I willing to work toward solving the conflict?

5. Would my parents have welcomed my effort to resolve family conflicts and be able to respond positively if I had ever made the first move?

6. What would my parents have done to improve our relationship if they had been willing?

7. What did I enjoy about my parents and in what ways am I like them or not like them?

If There Is a Preparation for Death, It Is Reparation with Parents before Their Deaths

The best preparation for death is reparation of the relationship. If there is a way to prepare for the death of your parents it is to do as much repair work as you can on your relationship with them. Most of us could certainly have enjoyed better relationships with our parents. We could have had better communication, spent more meaningful time together, and enjoyed our precious moments without conflict or strife. It is good to resolve conflicts after parents die (better than not at all) but it is also good to resolve them before they die. The best preparation for their eventual deaths is reparation with them before they die.

When thinking about how to make an effort to solve problems with parents, it helps to be willing to let go of angry feelings and to take risks. For example, you have a long-standing fury about how your father pushed you to go into the family business. When you tried it and hated it, he felt you weren't trying hard enough. When you went on to do something else, he constantly harped on the fact that the business would not continue after his death.

Can you be mature enough to accept your father for who he is and understand why he felt as he did? If you can, those old wounds he inflicted are more likely to heal, and you will be able to forgive and forget. Understand that he is less than perfect—and so are you. That should make it easier for you to accept him for who he is, just as you would have liked him to accept you for who you are. Acceptance is the key. It is a model for what is frequently referred to these days as "unconditional love."

The ultimate act is that of accepting yourself. If you can come to accept yourself first, you can then open up a line of communication with a parent with whom there has been some problem. Self-acceptance makes it possible for you to say to your parent, "I would like it if you could tell me why you feel so strongly about . . ." Your own self-acceptance allows your parent's opinion to be no more than that: just an opinion. You already accept yourself, and the parent's opinion cannot change that self-acceptance. But that parent's opinion might allow you to know, and eventually accept, the parent more fully.

The work you do to heal your wounds and fix troubled parental relationships is vitally important. If you can find a way to love instead of feeling anger toward your parents, you free up time and energy that is otherwise spent on overcoming the resentment you feel when your parents die and you are alone. You are bound to change; that is the nature of the psychology of grief. Whether or not change results in renewal depends on how much you are willing to do your work.

The case of Michael, age 46, a writer and producer of documentaries, is a good example of rapprochement. He took action by using a method he called constructive communications to deal with his grief. He wrote a series of private and unpublished dialogues for the other members of his support group, the purpose of which was to encourage healthy interactions between the bereaved and their deceased parents. The dialogues encouraged communication, hearing, and listening.

Additionally these dialogues taught individuals how to speak with one another during the time of illness and death. They were intended to be good for everyone, parents and adult children alike. In fact, these conversations are positive for everyone in the family, including siblings, aunts, and grandchildren. Often, it takes more than one conversation to improve the quality of these parent-adult child or family relationships.

Loving Takes Guilt and Regret Out of the Grieving Process

It is not easy to put aside your feelings about what your parent did or didn't provide for you. It is not easy to forget your hurts, disappointments and failures. Now, the best thing you can do for yourself—and for your parents—is to try to get over whatever still bothers you. Hopefully you will be able to get past blaming them for difficulties you have had in your own life.

Developing a somewhat fatalistic attitude about your elderly parents may be helpful in combating blame. By fatalistic, I mean that you realize that their death may be imminent and there is not much they can do to initiate communication. Mending bridges or changing their ways may be impossible at this point if they have not been successful at it in the past. However, it is the last chance you will have to say things that need to be said, so you will want to try to say them. Then forgive, forget, and move on before they die. You will benefit if you can take responsibility for this healing effort and come to a loving, compassionate attitude toward them.

How well one manages loss is affected by:

➤ The nature of the survivor's relationship with the person who has died

➤ The personality of the survivor

➤ The surrounding social circumstances

➤ The individual's psychological reactions to bereavement

➤ The feelings of duty to the deceased

Recovery from grief is affected by:

➤ Ambivalent feelings toward the deceased

➤ Unresolved conflicts with the deceased

➤ Dependency upon the deceased

Breaking the Ice

If you are someone who has a history of conflict with a parent, yet you would like to mend your relationship before your parent dies, there are small steps you can take to break the ice, especially if the parent is failing:

1. Discuss the parent with a sibling or other relative to determine the likelihood of his or her being receptive to your approach.

2. Assess the needs of the parent with another person.

3. Write a letter to the parent. (If it takes on an angry tone, you don't have to send it, but writing an unsent letter can help clear the decks to writing another, less polemic one that can be sent.)

4. Mail a picture of any grandchildren.

5. If both of your parents are alive, speak to the one you are closest to.

6. Assess the situation again.

7. Send flowers.

8. Send the parent's favorite food.

9. Try to create a team effort for care giving between family members and/or health-care providers.

10. Express your intention of breaking the ice to your parent.

John, age 38, comments, "My father and I never got along and I didn't see him much after his divorce from my mother. He would call occasionally from Texas where he moved after he remarried, but he had more children and I think he didn't want to be bothered with me. I was always mad at my mother for how she handled family matters after the divorce as well, and after college I moved away and settled down with a woman from a large family with whom I closely bonded.

"When my mother became sick, her sister took care of her. I began to feel so guilty, and my wife suggested that if nothing else, I should call once a month or send something nice to her. I knew it wasn't enough, because, after all, she was my mother. But, there had been such a wall between us, I didn't know if I could break through it even though she was dying. My wife would go shopping and buy my mother a nightgown to wear in the hospital. It seems like such a small thing to do. It made me feel a little better. But, then after she died, and I went to her funeral, I broke down and cried one day because I had never really opened up to her. Now it was too late. I will probably be left with this void in me for the rest of my life. . . . That's just how it is."

Max, age 57, says, "By the time I realized I needed to get over my rage at my father, it was too late. He was so debilitated by senility that he could barely carry on a conversation with me. I wonder if he didn't lose his mind because he was never able to talk to any of us like normal people. He was always criticizing us for one thing or another. Nothing was ever right for him. Hard to believe my sister and I grew up to be normal at all. We got absolutely no affection from him. He was such a cold man. Before his death, Natalie, my sister, and I decided to try to forgive him despite what a monster he had been. We formed a strong alliance between the two of us and took turns doing what we could for him. I can tell you honestly, nothing came from the heart, but we managed to care for him a little. Whatever we did helped, because at his funeral Natalie hugged me and said, 'We have always been on our own, but at least we did something for the man whose life is responsible for ours. I couldn't have lived with myself if I had just let him die with no attention from us.' I agreed."

Saying Good-bye with Rituals

There is good reason for cleaning up relationships with parents before they die. Communicating with them is part of this clean up. Unexpressed thoughts and feelings you wanted to share with your parents commonly cause frustration after their deaths. You can say whatever you want to your deceased parents after they are gone, and the words you speak can be very healing and will provide closure for you.

Part of preparing for the death of parents is thinking about how you would like to spend your last days with your parents. Many of my patients felt strongly that, had they been able to prepare for how they wanted to talk to their parents before they died, it would have resulted in a more helpful and healing outcome. For example, Marsha, age 52, said, "Now that my mother, who was the last parent to die, is gone, I think about how I would have benefited from having a planned discussion with her. Sort of like clearing the air. I would have talked about our relationship and what I loved about her. I would have asked her something very specific to me, like 'Why didn't you want me to go to drama school?' or 'What is your favorite thing about me?'"

After discussing similar issues with many people, I have come to the conclusion that creating a planned discussion (or even a ritualized ceremony of closure) with a dying parent can be beneficial. Not everyone may want to try this, but it has been effective. A fellow psychologist, age 55, said, "When my own mother died, we all gathered around her and had sort of a Thanksgiving ceremony for Mom. We each described what we had loved about Mom the most, how she had influenced each of us, what our favorite dinner had been, what we appreciated most about her. We each said 'I love you, thank you for being such a good mom,' and then we all sat around and listened to Beethoven, her favorite music. Days later, when she died, we all felt peaceful and complete."

What would have been on the list of things you would have wanted to say to your mother or father before they died? Saying good-bye in a well-planned way is a ritual. The preparations you make for your final conversations are rituals. Thinking beforehand about what you would like to finish before the parent dies is preparation for such a ritual. You might say such things as:

> ➤ I am happy you were my parent.

> ➤ I am happy we got closer later in life.

> ➤ I am happy we learned to express ourselves to each other.

> ➤ I loved you and appreciated what you did for me.

Good-bye conversations are just as much for the surviving child as they are for the parent who is about to die. Over the years, certain issues will have become apparent. The following possible beginnings for good-bye conversations reflect some of these issues.

For the Parent:

1. There is something I always wanted to ask you and always wanted to know. Our time is running out and here is my question . . .

2. There is something I always wanted to say to you . . .

3. I always wanted to tell you this about me . . .

For the Adult Child:

1. What did you appreciate about me?

2. Do you have advice for me in the future?

3. Did you know that I felt . . . ?

4. If we could have communicated better, I would have said . . .

5. I am sorry if I ever made you feel . . .

And, if possible:

6. This is how I really felt about the time when you . . .

7. I forgive you for the times you . . .

Consciously facing the thought of your parents' death is becoming widely practiced these days because it serves an important function. It allows for everyone in the partnership to say what he or she needs to say when it matters most, at the end of someone's life. Although it can be painful, it is good prevention. Your life will not be haunted with regret if you can say the things that probably live within your mind or heart.

My patient Connie was 37 when her mother died. Their relationship had been fairly close, but Connie moved away with her husband in her late twenties and from that time only saw her mother two to three times a year. They spoke often, but it was not Connie who was responsible for care giving during her mother's final illness. That responsibility was left for the two siblings who remained at home.

Connie felt that moving away from home was her first separation from her parents and family. She described her relationships with her parents as close, but she didn't mind raising her own children away from them. It always seemed to me that she had a wealth of unresolved feelings and issues, in particular with her mother. This proved to be the case when her mother died, and she called me and wanted to see me for a few sessions. Connie complained about having low energy, and at the same time she was restless and irritable. I assured her that these were all symptoms of normal grief, and that she was also mildly depressed because of her unresolved feelings about the loss. We began discussing how she had felt about her mother. It became clear that Connie had not fully experienced or expressed the love she felt inside for her. This made Connie feel worse rather than better.

Connie finally realized that what was most upsetting to her was that she had never told her mother how much she loved her. This caused Connie to experience a great deal of sorrow, and she cried copiously in therapy with me. I instructed Connie to write her deceased mother a letter, pretend her mother was in the room or go to her grave and talk to her. However, a conversation with her mother in real life is the only thing that would have appeased her in that moment, and such a conversation was now impossible. I attempted to make Connie recognize that her expression of these emotions would help her cope with her very intense feelings. In time, I hope Connie found relief.

In contrast, Connie's sister, Brenda, who lived in closer proximity to their mother, described a very different, more peaceful experience, all of which heightened Connie's feelings of remorse. Brenda, who was responsible for caregiving, saw their mother every day. (This happens so often within a family—the siblings who live near the parent become responsible for caregiving instead of the responsibilities being shared equally among all the children in a family.) Brenda naturally had plenty of time to talk with their mother about everything—her mother's upbringing, family values, religion, her father, her grandparents, how she wanted to be buried, what she wanted to wear to be buried in, the things her mother worried about, how their mother wanted her property dispersed, and her wish for all of her children to be happy after she was gone.

Saying Good-bye Privately

The nature of the contact Brenda had with her mother demonstrates another positive aspect of saying good-bye. An opportunity to have privacy with the parent is important to facilitate each child's separate communication with the parent. As the child speaks individually with the parent before death, an intimacy is created—perhaps for the first time in the relationship. This intimacy is wonderful for the child and can also give comfort in a conscious and loving way to the parent who is facing death. Simply to feel there are no "loose ends" with a child can help the parent find a sense of serenity at the end of his or her life.

Michel, age 63, described his mother's death as graceful. Michel, a therapist, had worked professionally in the field of hospice care and was quite comfortable dealing with a person's last stage of life:

> For days before Mom died, we held each other and talked openly about whatever came to our minds. It was a lovely experience. She would cry, I would cry, we would laugh and hug each other. Of course, she wasn't the perfect mother. Who is? But it didn't matter, because I knew she would be leaving soon, and I wanted it to be as good as possible for both of us. I held no grudges, she held nothing back. She told me she felt badly for leaving, and I assured her I felt no abandonment. She was sick, and she had to die. I was sad but didn't want her to continue to suffer. Now that she has been gone for a year, I recall that final conversation with great detail and feel thankful we were fortunate to have had it. I might have been left with such a terrible feeling of burden otherwise. It could have ruined what was left of my own life.

Having the opportunity to deal with painful issues before parents die is very useful. For those of you with parents already deceased, this section will not be relevant. However, in case you know someone who has not yet lost his or her parent, you may want to share some of this. It is good preventive medicine.

"To Thine Own Self Be True"

Shakespeare's admonition is truly significant during the adult orphan's journey because it is the star that lights your way now and guides you comfortably in a direction that should be familiar at its best and adventuresome at its least. Your own shining inner light, your core, or essence is what you have to fall back on, now that your parent's world and your parents are no longer with you.

This inner core, or self, is familiar. Most of you have been in touch for all of your lives with what you call your inner self. But, the self within a family system and the self without a family system is a *different* self, and this is clearly obvious when you are in the position you are now in—without parents.

You existed as your parent's child for many years. You lived in a world with your parents that created a joint environment which orchestrated the first movement of the symphony you call your life. Think of the volume of information that passed through your experience of your life with your parents, beginning in your infancy and continuing until their deaths. How can you minimize the impact of all that?

Now the time has come for you to live again, in a new way, and in a way that can be exciting, rewarding, and fulfilling. Let yourself do your grief work and be reborn on the other side of your loss into what can be a new you. The time has come for a second movement in your life. Take charge of this movement as the conductor who oversees all of your beautiful aspects and come to know yourself as if for the first time. Find something new about yourself and make it something you just love!

3

The Self Explodes:
Reclaiming the Self

*Man is asked to make of Himself what he is supposed
to become to fulfill his destiny.*

—Paul Tillich

Accepting the need to grieve begins your process of dealing with
loss. Not dealing with grief is an option but it is one without
much personal benefit to you. By allowing yourself to feel your feelings, you will receive immediate positive results because being so in
touch with yourself is empowering. Grieving is hard work—but it
pays off.

As you grieve, you turn yourself over to the unexpected. In so
doing, there is a natural shift from rationality to creativity as you
begin to "let go" to whatever comes. For example, one individual
shared these feelings: "I did not know how long I would cry in the
car or sob unexpectedly when I saw someone who looked like my
dad. I was shocked by how much feeling I had about my dad when
he died, and I was surprised by how much my daily responsibilities
ceased to matter compared to my wanting to mourn without anything interfering."

After loss there is an immediate period of shock and emotional
upheaval, followed by a figurative search for your lost parent. While your

immediate tendency might be to push away strong feelings like sadness and pain, it is far more positive to stay open. The next stage you will feel is chaos and disorientation, and you must be patient. It will not last forever. This is the time for you to experience whatever feeling, idea about the relationship, or image of your parent that surfaces.

Your need to control the experience is overshadowed by your intent to "go with the flow." Your willingness to surrender to the potential for movement and creativity will help you to progress to the next stage of grief, which is reorganization of your life. By the time reorganization occurs, you will be different and more willing to receive a piece of information about yourself.

When I began to research the effects of parental death on adult children several years ago, I was surprised. First, there was very little accurate information. Second, the information that did exist was biased. Common wisdom at the time minimized the effects of parental death because it was considered to be a normal and expected life event. The tendency was to suggest to adults that they "just get over it already" and resume their regular lives as though untouched by this major life event.

Fortunately, times have changed and parental death is now seen as an important life transition, signaling the end of childhood and the passage into full maturity. Realizing the rich potential for personal growth justifies the suffering and bereavement you feel. There are many benefits to conscious grief. The following are some of the most important:

> ➤ Adaptation to your loss can make you stronger and more complete.

> ➤ Feeling your pain is hard but will promote knowing yourself.

> ➤ Acceptance of your creative impulse motivates you to keep going.

> ➤ Loss and grief can be positive catalysts for change.

> ➤ The necessary focus on yourself will help you achieve the new goals you set for yourself.

Research suggests that grieving for parents needs to be examined in a new light—one that recognizes the value of the points I just made.[1] It may be the case that the final stage of grief, commonly called recovery, is a period of life that lasts much longer than was earlier thought, perhaps even until the end of your own life.

Recovery is a dynamic period of change, characterized by your developing new meaning in your life, new personal goals, reclaimed aspects of your personality, a new self-concept. The challenge is to "stay" with the grief feelings until they have naturally transformed themselves into something useful and inspiring. You are encouraged to understand the meaning of parental loss in a new way, one that will lead you to opening yourself to the possibilities naturally available.

Although the grieving process is vitally important, this book is not about grief. It is about where grief can take you. It is a book about life—in particular, the renewal of life you can experience as your grieving turns into new beginnings and personal discovery. The goal is transformation resulting from:

➤ Personal introspection

➤ Motivation to enjoy life after loss

➤ Intent to cope without parents and bring gain to experience of loss

➤ Honoring the parent who died

The Unexplored Self

What part of your self is recovered or discovered? Is it something that is familiar? Is it something you knew about yourself but hid because of conditioning, tradition, morals, values, insecurity, fear, lack of commitment, self-doubt, lack of encouragement? Or was something about your self vague, shadowy, unclear, formless? Perhaps you have been unfamiliar or uncomfortable with thinking about your self too much, as though it was "not nice to be overly self-involved."

What you may recover as parts of self may have lain dormant for any of the above reasons. It is your loss that allows you to recover these parts. Yet, they are available now and you can contact them through deep concentration, meditation, questioning. For example, imagine yourself quiet and peaceful. Let something surface about you or a way of being or responding that you've not let out before.

> Michael, age 30 and a massage therapist, said, "When my father died I did what the Native Americans do at important times in their lives, they would go to the sweat lodge and get in touch with themselves. I needed time to be alone and to think about myself and how I felt after losing my dad. How was I going to change? I asked. What would be different for me now?"

The Self Explodes

Some individuals described what happened to them after their parents died as an explosion of feelings. These people felt everything! They felt tumult, excitation, exhilaration, and endless possibility, in addition to the typical feelings of grief and loss.

> A woman, age 50, said, "There were 'endless me's' dying to come out; the me that wanted to travel, the me that wanted to sing, the me who wanted to scream when I was angry, the me who wanted to adopt more children, the me who wanted to hold onto the children I had harder and with more passion. Where had I been all my life? Why haven't I been out before?"

Self-image changes first, followed by self-expression, which brings self-actualization.

What you are capable of finding is your own true self, your real essence and however it wants to express itself. Your true self has existed from birth and lives deep within what you call your center. It is your essence and it contains your personality, nature, goals, purpose, talents. Beneath the surface of what you were accustomed to believing was your *only* self, is more self, full of insight and inspiration about your identity (who you really are). It is the self that explodes when you are orphaned and it contains what's been hidden about you; what you knew about yourself and hid, or what you didn't know or were afraid of.

Self psychologists call it the *true self* or the *authentic self* and it awaits discovery. Certainly you can remember times when aspects of your true self were seen and were not met with great excitement by others. If it was your parents who showed little enthusiasm for whatever you were doing, you may have begun a process of suppression. Michelle, age 40, said, "I can remember dancing for my parents and they didn't smile or laugh, and then I just stopped."

Your true self also contains whatever about you is artistically creative. This self defines, presents, and reveals your identity and listening to it is rewarding. Whether your creative side wants to use words, paint, dance, act, write, or perform, it deserves to be noticed. If you have been resistant to allowing your creative side out, let it out!

Selfhood *from Childhood*

You were born into an already existing system called your family. In order to function within your family system, you may have relinquished some part of your individual nature to fit in. In addition, rules about behavior and the expression of feeling may have affected your level of comfort in being yourself. In some families, anger is not acceptable; in others, discussions about sexuality. For your family to function, you probably had to adapt to what was considered acceptable within it and you learned to suppress what wasn't. If you didn't care about being acceptable, or "good," your behavior would have been different and you might have been seen by your parents or siblings as rebellious or "bad."

Did you feel you could be yourself within your family? To what extent? Did you feel you were accepted for yourself? Valued for yourself? Would your parents support who you were, despite their own feelings? Did you choose friends or a career based on your own sense of self? Did you identify and choose hobbies based on your truest self?

How would you describe your success as an individual while your parents were alive? How has that changed now that they are gone?

How would you describe your parents' role in helping you to become:

- ➤ Independent?
- ➤ Self-sufficient?
- ➤ Self-motivating and self-directed?
- ➤ Self-expressive?
- ➤ Autonomous?
- ➤ Self-reliant?
- ➤ Accomplished?
- ➤ Self-actualized?
- ➤ Self-aware?
- ➤ Resourceful?
- ➤ Inner-directed?

Were you encouraged to explore your life by making your own decisions; setting your own goals; expressing your true feelings, thoughts, and ideas; becoming what you wanted to be?

Did you depend on your parents to encourage your independence, or did you become that way in spite of it all?

Were your goals and talents appreciated, accepted, and reinforced by your parents and family? Were you encouraged to:

- ➤ Fit in?
- ➤ Conform?
- ➤ Be like your parents?
- ➤ Do as your parents said?
- ➤ Follow in their footsteps?

➤ Adjust to family traditions?

➤ Stay in the family?

➤ Not wander outside the boundaries of what the family expected?

➤ Make your goals their goals, or make their goals your goals?

Did your parents ever say to you:

➤ Do whatever makes you happy.

➤ Seek individual freedom.

➤ Be yourself.

➤ Don't do what I say, do what you want to do.

➤ Please both of us, but please yourself first.

➤ Hear me, but don't listen unless it's right for you.

Or did your parents say:

➤ In our family, we do this . . .

➤ We expect you to . . .

➤ You could never succeed at . . .

➤ If only you would listen to us and . . .

➤ You think you know what is right for you, but we know better; we are older, wiser, and so on

➤ You are not good enough to . . .

Your parents may very well have been a liability because of their:

➤ Negligence

➤ Lack of reinforcement

➤ Lack of inspiration

➤ Criticisms

➤ Lack of enthusiasm for your talent

➤ Practicality

➤ Expectations

➤ Limited world view

➤ Antipathy for your potential

➤ Envy or jealousy

➤ Overprotectiveness

➤ Love for another sibling

➤ Love for another family member

➤ Lack of nurturing ability

Did you do what you wanted anyway? Many did.

In spite of the lack of parental respect for individuality, many people felt as though they always did what they wanted to do.

Maria, age 60 and a nurse, was determined her entire life to work in the medical profession and wanted to be a physician. But, her father believed that Maria should just get married and have children. She raged for years about her father's lack of enthusiasm for her own career interests. She wanted more in life than being married and having children. She had goals and a strong personal need for accomplishment.

It was difficult for Maria to pay for her own education, and her father refused to help her. She had several jobs, and it took her longer to complete her education but her determination allowed her to reach her goal.

But, her father never helped her to succeed—either emotionally or financially. When her brothers expressed the desire to go to college and graduate school, he was pleased and did everything in his power to support their goals. When Maria spoke up, her father was mute. No help, no support, no school. Maria graduated high school and began to support herself. She never went to college and never became a doctor. Eventually, she studied at night school, taking courses whenever she could, and did finally become a nurse. "My dad never helped me, and for that I will always resent him," she says.

Mike, age 30 and an adult orphan, said, "My dad thwarted every goal I had. Any time I would come to him with an idea, he would say, 'Don't expect a lot of yourself. Just get a job and make money.' In spite of him, I became quite successful in business, and he seemed surprised by my efforts. He just could never accept that his son was going to make something great out of himself. After I did, he bragged to his friends that I have money, but I sure didn't have any of his support when I needed it. And he called himself my father! What kind of a father derails you every chance he gets?"

Joe, age 40, a man who has still not "found himself," describes always feeling misunderstood in his family: "I was always the odd man out; I was too sensitive for my father; I didn't have the skills my other brother had; and I wasn't smart like my sister. I tried to express my frustrations to my parents, but no one seemed to listen. I moved out after high school and floundered for years. When my parents died I felt relief that my struggle with them was over; guilt because I had not been closer to them; fear that I would not have money to fall back on; pity for my siblings who were really sad; freer to find other people to become close to; and determined to find something I enjoyed doing."

The Birth Self

The birth self is the natural essence of who you are. It is part of your innate nature. Parents recognize clear evidence of a child's individual selfhood right from birth. It is reflected in your natural abilities, talents, nature, temperament, personality, likes, dislikes, moods, wants, needs. You are guided and formed by your parents, family, society, and culture. While your parents were alive, your goal was probably to balance pleasing yourself and pleasing your parents. How much of your birth self was lost in this effort?

Some of you will admit that "you could have been more yourself." By that I mean you could have benefited in your life if you had been able to better express qualities, abilities, and traits you felt were truly your own—your *birth self.* You will also be able to recognize that your ability to more completely express those aspects of your self would have been aided if you had enjoyed more independence and freedom. When your parents are gone, you are going to be able to begin living your life without their influence and without the need to fit into your family system. You will be liberated to begin your "search for your birth self"—the self that is uniquely your own and free from the influence of your parents—and to decide for yourself whether or not it is being fully expressed in the world.

Middle Age

Despite the trials and tribulations of maturation, each of you developed, matured, and prospered as adults. You developed into young adulthood and then eventually into middle age. One issue you face when you reach middle age is how to reaffirm your sense of self while illuminating the deepest truths about your nature.

According to Carl Jung, middle age is about reevaluating life anyway.[2] Middle-age values and ideals change as the relentless fact of growing older becomes apparent. Your physical body changes, your sex and aggression drives slow down from a roar to a hum, and you begin to think about existential values. You ask what matters now. You have become part of the sandwich generation—a caregiver for the preceding and following generations. Being "yourself" may not matter as much as taking care of your responsibilities.

Losing your parents in middle age means they were present for you when you had your own children. The gift of having grandparents for your children and an extended family is worth self-sacrifice for a period of time, if that is what's necessary. When your parents are gone, it is for a long time.

It is true that it has taken a great deal of time for attention to be focused on the impact of parental death. This is at least partially because of the notion that it is expected and that it often does occur when the adult child is middle aged. In middle age there are so many other issues that a person might be dealing with that the death of a parent who is relatively old and not the focus of daily life should simply be taken in stride. Nothing could be further from the truth.

The Loss of Parents Is Different from Any Other Loss

A groundbreaking study by C. M. Parkes introduced a humanistic approach to grief and became the basis for further study of bereavement in widows.[3] No longer was grief minimized. The depth of pain and acceptance of the process were recognized. Even though this model of coping with grief began as a study of individuals who had lost spouses, it soon generalized to the loss of all loved ones, including the loss of parents, despite the inevitability of their deaths.

Such an accepting approach to grief allows the grief to exist and the grief feelings to be acceptable and honored. In contrast to the traditional view of grief as something to be gotten over quickly, what emerged was the recognition of the seriousness of grief and loss. Now it was possible to focus on the emotional problems survivors encountered following death. These problems included weeping, anxiety, sleeplessness, restlessness, a desire to join the lost individual, difficulty in coping with life, and uncertainty about being able to return to a normal existence.

Orphaned adults need those around them to recognize and pay attention to the depth and profundity of the loss. People often mention that they most want to have those they love acknowledge that their loss was significant. This acknowledgment and the contingent support are a way of respecting and paying homage to the parent who has been lost. In addition, many people report a change in the hierarchy of familial relationships, with adult children becoming more significant in the care of the widow or widower and of younger children.

Finally, many people reported a need for closer familial relationships. As Emma, age 45, put it, "I found myself finally becoming a real aunt to my niece. She had had a hard life and had lost her mother, my sister, not too long before the death of my father, her grandfather. Oh, I guess we used to talk on the phone once in a great while. Now, we talk almost weekly, and I think it has been a help to both of us."

We all learn from experience that the risk of forming relationships in which we become very attached is the loss of the relationship when the person leaves or when we leave. But the situation is different with parents. As you have matured into adults, separation from your parents necessarily meant you would move away physically and emotionally. In the family, it was assumed this was a positive step. But even as we grow up and move away, we still continue to be our parents' children and to have a relationship with them, whether positive, complicated, or difficult. "What is important is that some time in our life we must face and deal with loss and separation."[4]

It is obvious that when separation occurs because of death, we will grieve and we will suffer. No matter how complex or conflicted the parental relationship, not one of the people I interviewed was immune to the experience of grief and loss. Although being launched into life on your own as an adult is considered to be a positive step, parental death, in its ultimate finality, declares to the orphaned adult, "You are now on your own." So, at first, shock, sorrow, and confusion occupy the grieving adult. But eventually, the human need to replace loss with the life force begins to take hold.

Reconnecting to creativity (life force) and the impulse to live fully are the organic consequences of coping with loss. Your own death is now nearer and your looming mortality urges you onward to construct a new self. "Not only does the loss of a parent force the child to face death, but also face its polar opposite: life and personal growth. Death of parents may usher in a sense of needing to reorganize the self as a way to deal with the profound impact of the loss. What is desired is a feeling of autonomy that flows from a deep sense of one's own identity."[5]

In my research, I have found that no one is emotionally prepared to release a parent when death occurs. Intellectualize all we want, there is no way to know what the loss will really feel like until it occurs. These findings are concurrent with the works of Weiss,[6] Bowlby,[7] and Parks.[8] As you begin the grieving process, it is important to remember you are not alone. Many of my patients made it very clear that sharing their grief with other family members was a way of connecting with the living while grieving for the dead. You should feel entitled to:

➤ Look for as much support as you feel you need.

➤ Give yourself time to grieve.

Obviously, the closer the relationship between you and your parent, the greater will be the tie or attachment, and the greater the loss. Basically, if the parent you have lost played a very traditional parenting role in your life, caring for your physical needs in childhood and adolescence, you will have little desire for such nurturing in middle age. However, if you had a deeper intellectual relationship with your parent, you may have maintained a significant bond with the parent into middle age. "[This bond is] a dynamic bio-social one which persists throughout life."[9]

Clearly, the person who has taken control of his or her own life has the ability to respect the bond to the parent even after death, without letting this impede their progress in life. And this tie or bond to the parent need not be an impediment that keeps us in the past, but a part of the human condition, which, by nature, must join past and present to maintain the possibility of progress in life.

Among other differences between losing a parent and losing other close relatives is that with our parents we come to expect and accept that they will pass away before we do. Add to this the present phenomenon of deteriorating marital relationships that has resulted in a divorce rate of 50 percent or more. When there is marital trouble, parents who are close to their adult married children often come through for them in very positive ways, and this support may also be missed after a parent you are close to passes away.

The people I interviewed had varying responses to parental death according to the intensity of their family ties. The closer the family, the deeper the loss. Cultural traditions and religious beliefs may also intensify family bonds and deepen attachment and, therefore, loss. In addition, if you have strong family ties and a good social support structure in place, your grieving will be made easier. If the financial resources of both yourself and your deceased parent are comfortable, your practical concerns will weigh less heavily upon you as you grieve and adapt.

Louise, age 53, put it more simply when she told me with a quizzical smile, "I've always had this on-again, off-again, good, bad, wacky relationship with my dad. Also, he was disabled and failing for a couple of years prior to his death, so I had the time and the emotional distance to prepare. Or so I thought. Fat chance. Boy was I amazed at how deep I felt my loss. I felt pretty sheepish about that. I had wanted to be oh so stoic in front of my friends, and even though I feel it, I still don't talk about it much."

As she worked to put her astonishment at her feelings into words, she went on to say, "I found out there is no preparing for death. And it's the finality that overwhelms the most. He's gone, and I have to believe it, but it's still unbelievable. It's like suddenly discovering the world is flat after all by falling off the edge."

Integrating Your Loss

The impact of the death of your parent brings you to a real examination of mortality and how you relate to it. Here are some of the milestones along this emotional journey:

1. Initially, the parental bond appears severed.

2. You begin a life review with the image of your parent in mind.

3. You attempt to recapture the essence of your parent.

4. Memories and past events are recalled.

5. Disappointments, frustrations, and guilty feelings may come to mind.

6. You confront the loss of the source of your own nativity.

7. You may tend to dwell on negative aspects of recollections about your parents.

8. Eventually, you adjust to the situation, resolving questions such as: "Was I loved?" "Was I understood?" "Was I good enough?" "Did they ever really approve of me?"

9. You begin to feel orphaned, and you develop strengths and courage.

10. You have faced their death and survived.

Recent studies acknowledge the likelihood of change to the sense of self after parental loss. "Death is both a loss and a life course transition for the adult child, specifically the effect of parent death on the adult child's perceptions of self, personal continuity, and well-being."[10] The majority of those I interviewed reported changes in their perception of their own maturity. Personal priorities and career objectives were often reconsidered and adjusted. Needless to say, every person I spoke with noted the impact of losing a parent on his or her own sense of mortality. When you lose a parent or both parents in middle age it is also important to note that the loss coincides with midlife issues, such as trying to strike the balance of personal autonomy and freedom with that of responsibility. Many people told me that the loss of the parent helped spur them on to resolving such midlife issues more quickly and completely. In general, people told me that parental loss helped them reach a greater level of self-confidence and that, at the same time, they found themselves to be just as responsible or more responsible than they were before. My own findings are corroborated by the work of Andrew Scharlach and Karen Fredriksen, who conducted interviews with 83 adults aged 35 to 60 who had lost a parent within five years of the interview. They found that fully 60 percent of those interviewed continued during that time to experience emotional reactions to these deaths and 44 percent continued to experience somatic reactions to the death.[11] The changes in self-concept reported by this study also indicate a general shift in self-perception and confirm the possibility of an even deeper change on the emotional, psychological, and developmental levels.

Historically, experiencing the death of a loved one has been viewed as a completely negative experience. However, new information suggests that there are positive aspects of bereavement—even when the loss is of a parent. There is an indication that loss can lead to personal growth, adult development, and self-transformation. My work and the studies I consulted all take note of the additional possibility that parental loss can lead to a greater ability to take risks and a greater understanding of human connectedness. The death of your parents can be what helps you to create a new philosophy of life and leads you to a heightened sense of who you are and what matters to you.

Monica was 47 years old when her last parent died. She suggested the establishment of a place where adults who had lost their parents might retreat to reevaluate how different their existence might be as a result of their loss. When her father died, leaving her orphaned, Monica reported an awakened seriousness about life and her own life's role. She asked herself, "What am I doing with my life? What am I using my life for?"

She defined her next task in life as trying to discover something new about herself that she was committed to developing more fully. She called her commitment to self-discovery her "transitional fertile period." Monica posed herself difficult internal questions that she then analyzed and worked hard on. I thought the idea of orphan fertility was interesting and encouraged her to think about it. Monica had begun a second career as a stockbroker, but she had always been interested in becoming a writer. She began interviewing her friends who had become orphaned and wrote essays describing all of their experiences.

We isolated a number of interesting themes that her friends had in common:

➤ Life was beginning again.

➤ This renewal was important.

➤ The value of life had increased.

➤ The value of existing relationships had increased.

➤ Self-discovery as an orphan allowed a fresh look at yourself, specifically because you were alone and had no parents.

➤ The inhibiting effect of parental opinion about lifestyle choices ended.

➤ The inhibition directly affected one's sense of self, and this is what was now being transformed.

➤ The natural direction of the transformation was to become more inner-directed.

➤ The transformation resumed where you had left off at an earlier stage in life.

Think of knitting a sweater. You knit a portion of it but still have a lot to do, and at some point, you put it down. Then your parents die. You return to your knitting and finish the sweater. That is the process of beginning to be more of who you are. This is the living example of what has been called the "developmental push."[12] You are enabled to resume your own personal development at whatever place you were stopped earlier in life, and those I have interviewed confirm this.

Bill, age 29, expressed it this way: "I can take control of my own life. I am going to have to control situations I never controlled before, because my parents did it for me, like taking care of money and investments."

Michael, age 56, commented, "If I am going to control my own life now, boy, I am going to do things so differently. For example, I am going to stop going to church. It never felt right to me. I went to please my parents. Now I am not going. I feel more spiritual than ever, but have no interest in formal religion."

It is important to remember that change affects everyone differently. For Michael, giving up formalized religion became an important change. Tom, age 35, decided to renew his religious connection. While his parents were alive, they forced him to accompany them to temple and he acquiesced. After their deaths, he wanted to go, out of a need to maintain a symbolic connection to his parents.

Rediscovery of yourself can help you reclaim a feeling, a way of expressing emotion, a value, a personal attribute, a way of thinking, a talent, a specific element of your personality. All of these make you special and define you as an individual. Some newly recovered behaviors might include:

- ➤ A sense of humor

- ➤ A more affectionate nature

- ➤ An ability to control impulsive/compulsive behavior

- ➤ Ability to develop closer relationships

- ➤ Greater/lesser motivation for success

- ➤ Greater need for closeness with children

- ➤ Ability to overcome shyness

- ➤ Ability to be more aggressive/assertive

After your parent or parents die, you refocus your attention solely on yourself. You look, you seek, you explore, you direct your attention to your inner being. What are you feeling, you ask yourself? Who have you been? Who are you becoming?

Terry, age 57, a writer, says, "Many years after being orphaned, I see that I am more myself, and paradoxically less upset if my needs don't get met. There is a subtle sense of calm that has set in, a sense that I will be okay no matter what, and that my attachments to the outcomes of certain situations are no longer as important as in the past." Terry prides herself on this change. She describes herself as having been a control freak in the past. "Nothing was out of my sight and I needed to control as much as I could. Now, I see the bigger picture, and being right, or calling people on their stuff just doesn't matter as much. Now I am interested in life being smooth, easy, and as conflict-free as possible.

"I guess you might say I have transcended my ego and my need for control. Life is short, and I don't want to waste energy on other people's ego problems or needs to be powerful, rich, or successful. Let everyone handle their own stuff."

To find yourself orphaned at any age is to find yourself with the unique ability to find your own genius. Once you establish the nature of your self at orphanhood you can go about finding all of its aspects. The new selfhood that arises out of losing your parents presents itself as a vital force. I have spoken to many orphaned adults who have discovered extraordinary new talents and found the capacity to meet the challenge of putting creative dreams into action. Marvin Eisenstadt's research has documented this phenomenon. He describes orphanhood as providing a "will to power."[13]

Your new self emerges as you progress along the following sequence of tasks:

➤ Mourn the loss of parents.

➤ Reassess the lost relationships.

➤ Withdraw energy from parents.

➤ Live your own life.

➤ Create and develop new goals.

There is an immediate space or void created by your loss. What will fill it? How will you live without parents? While intellectually you realize you should no longer be dependent on your parents, emotionally you feel like the rug has been pulled out from under you. Depending on the quality of your attachment, you may suffer pain, distress, numbing, anger, feelings of isolation, confusion. You must say to yourself, I am alone now and I must develop the ability to care for myself. I have only myself to depend on now.

As time passes, you begin to assess how you feel about yourself. It is the tip of the iceberg. Questions arise from the depths of your mourning and soul-searching. Have you been living your life based on limitation, restricting the expression of some true aspect of yourself? If so, what are the aspects of your personality that have been hidden? Can they emerge now? What were your personal role and the role of your parents in this event? Have you responded with needs to please, to accommodate, to conform? These questions and many others contribute to the life crisis that occurs when parents die.

You begin to recognize the possibility for growing again. You begin to see changes appear. Will these changes be acceptable to others? How will your siblings, children, spouse feel about them? Often a consideration for others is tempered by the driving need for personal change.

Listen to Maxine, age 43:

Oh, I was the perfect little girl, always doing what I was supposed to. Even as a young adolescent and into my adulthood, my own identity was always the rug under the table, the chairs, the lamps, the vases, you name it. My own identity was obscured by anything and everything I could think of. Was I a pleaser? You bet! I cannot even fathom what I would have been like if my life had been directed by some internal force. I acquiesced to the demands and needs of all of my family members. I considered their feelings at most times.

Boy was I in for a shock when my mom died. I was suddenly without a role in life. I stood at the funeral home and trembled, because I did not know what would give meaning to my life now. The two adults who mattered more than anyone to me, except for my own children, were now gone. Even my husband's importance paled in comparison. As a matter of fact, my husband always envied how I felt about my parents, and he always accused me of loving them more and taking care of their needs over his. He was right!

Right or wrong, there are always some people who never leave their parents and treat their own biological family better than the person they marry. I was one of those. After weeks of being stunned and numb, I began to recognize something growing within me that wanted to get out. My husband called it a little monster; my teenagers called it being selfish. You might call it being spoiled or too self-involved, but I called it becoming me—finally becoming me.

For example, I found myself feeling like I wanted to do things my way, like making decisions about how to spend a bit of my inheritance money. Or wanting to change how I looked somewhat. I wanted to lose weight, wear more make-up, and change the style of my clothes, for starters. I wanted to study the Tango and I made my husband come with me. I wanted to start attending art classes, and I wanted to do that alone, even though it threatened my husband!

I gave myself permission to do it all!

That's what happened after my mother died.

It is the inner desire to change that gives the adult orphan the motivation for further adult growth. The impulse for progress then works to transform mourning the parental tie into personal success. Thus, the changes you make in your life, large and small, are for your own sake, but are also a way of maintaining an intimacy with parental memories. In improving your life, you are honoring your parents.

This helps to explain the intimate relationship connecting mourning and the progression of change, transformation, and the discovery of a new self. The progression begins to develop as an adaptation to loss. What is born from this progression is as lovely as the birth of an infant. At the time of your last parent's death, you yourself give birth to your newly shaped self, by granting permission for its growth.[14]

Your transformation at this stage combines a process of reevaluation, which is normal at this time of life anyway, and a transforming process of self-growth. It is the growing that is beautiful. Growth at this juncture reinforces the will to survive the loss of parents with grace and purpose. It is a powerful thrust into the future. The past power of your parents has been replaced with self-power.

The Old Power of Parents

Parents clearly had an impact on your personality. Do any of these comments sound familiar?

➤ Don't be silly!

➤ Act your age!

➤ Calm down and stop that.

➤ If you do that again I am going to . . .

➤ Why can't you be like . . .

➤ Your brother/sister wouldn't be doing . . .

➤ How many times do I have to tell you stop . . .

➤ Be serious!

➤ I am going to tell your father.

➤ I'm not going to tell you this again.

Comments, both positive and negative, influenced you and helped to shape your personality. Reactions to your behavior did the same. Your personality already existed, and it was affected by parental attitudes. Genetics, environment, and learning all formed the arena in which you developed. There was an interaction between you and your parents that played the primary role in your everyday experience.

The Status of Relationships

By the time your parents die you will have experienced many forms of interpersonal and social relationships. By far, marriages will have been the most significant of those relationships, unless your parents died before you were married. Becoming orphaned may push you into a relationship—or a marriage if you are already in a close comfortable relationship.

Many orphans report that relationships they had prior to the loss of a parent change form once the death has occurred. This is not surprising, considering the sense of loneliness that comes with this loss. A patient named Martin, age 43, married after his last parent died. He described his three-year relationship with a woman as friendly, compatible, and comfortable. "I felt extremely lonely after my last parent died and felt marriage would improve this condition." His loss motivated him to marry.

Changes in relationships can be for good or bad. Conrad, age 64 when he lost his father, later established a relationship with a woman who was very much like the negative part of his father; critical, demanding, and unloving. Conrad, without conscious choice, found a replacement figure for his deceased father. This re-creating of a parental love object resulted from a conflict that had existed between Conrad and his father and might have been avoided if Conrad had improved the quality of the relationship with his father before the father's death. His efforts to improve his female relationship failed and his conflicts with his deceased father continued. Conrad's relationship ended in disaster two years after his father died. His attempt to fix one relationship by trying to fix a different one ended miserably.

Michele, age 48 and a divorcee, said this about her attempts to hide from her difficult relationship with her mother and her feelings of grief:

> I tried everything bad in the book—drugs, alcohol, promiscuity! It is amazing how little they worked. In the long run, I was forced to start therapy and take a serious look at my issues. My parents were both alcoholics and never succeeded at anything. I raised myself with the help of my maternal grandmother. When both of my parents died, I felt relief and freedom. They were never my parents. Yet, there was still loss, and this is what I resisted looking at. I realized I had suffered parental loss before the age of 15. I had lost them to liquor.
>
> My father had been verbally abusive. I coped by not listening to him. One day I was not connected to him at all. I did the same thing with my mother. It is not surprising I did not choose well when I married, either time. Their deaths

didn't affect my choice of partners; their lives did that. Yet when they were both deceased, I was much more motivated to resolve my issues with them so I could establish a different network of friends.

Other ways marriages or other relationships are affected by parental death are the following:

➤ How much support the spouse of the survivor gives

➤ How much the power shift affects the survivor in regard to making important decisions

➤ How the survivor values other family members

A New Experience of Self

By now you will have realized that you have changed. Or you are in a process of change. Day by day, there will be something new for you to think about or feel. Your sense of yourself is adapting to the world without your parents. That cushion has been removed. It is being replaced with your own inner strength. Your personality has taken on a new dimension. Your old self was living as someone's child, and your new self lives alone. The natural consequence is that you will assert more independence, and your personality will take on more breadth.

The change can affect you suddenly as though a shield has been lifted. It occurs automatically, without your thinking about it. The behavior and the change can often be unconscious.

Ask yourself these questions:

➤ Who was I then? (preorphanhood)

➤ Who am I now? (postorphanhood)

➤ What are the subtle changes I perceive about myself?

➤ What are some new pursuits that might interest me?

New Definition of Self

You also ask yourself these questions:

> ➤ Who am I as a person?

> ➤ Who am I in relationship to others?

> ➤ Who am I in relationship to the world?

How did you go about exploring yourself? Was your process a product of your intention? Did it spontaneously occur? Or both? Did you take notes? Did you share it with someone you value or trust? Was your "process of becoming" a natural evolution, or did you need to control it? How did you feel different?

Becoming Whole

Personal growth can begin as soon as your parent dies and continue for the rest of your life. Most important, you become whole because you reconnect to lost elements of your own personality that were either partially or substantially excluded from your life. These would include talents, reactions, favorite pastimes, inclinations, whatever makes you unique. You will be rediscovering parts of yourself. You will become whole as you reconnect to your lost parts.

When you realize that this is actually an aspect of mourning, you will be surprised. This is an opportunity allowing you to reach inward. When your parent dies, there is a death of the you whose life was intertwined with that parent and life now becomes about you living for yourself. Therefore you can:

> ➤ Learn about your potential

> ➤ Express your potential

> ➤ Recognize the value of life and human values

> ➤ Want to help other adults without parents through crisis

➤ Become a more sensitive person and parent

➤ Develop and utilize all your unique capabilities

All of this leads you toward satisfying the goal of becoming a self-actualized person. By learning how to seek a positive outcome from a stressful and even a traumatic life event you are enabled to bring to light the very essence of creative growth. In fact, this is a transformation, quite a powerful transformation, which can only occur at this juncture of your now completed adult life.

4

Bending the Bough:
Beginning to Change

Freedom's just another word, for nothin' else to lose,
and nothin' ain't worth nothin' but it's free.

—"Me and Bobby McGee"
Kris Kristofferson and Fred Foster (1969)

T o begin to change, you must understand the vital importance of attachment to survival. Attachment plays a role in all human relationships. Your ability to attach to someone begins in infancy and is the emotional underpinning of later adult relationships. It is part of your biology. It was through the instinctive process of attachment that you developed a bond with your mother and father. As an infant, your most basic survival needs depended on the care you received from your mother, in particular, for obvious reasons. You might have perished if not for your mother's own instinct to nurture you. You possessed a natural ability to elicit nurturing through behaviors like crying and other verbal signs of distress, which could alert your mother to your need.

Adaptation to Family Life

To fully grasp the impact of the loss of your parents, you need to comprehend the essential and primary nature of attachment. The intensity of your attachment to your parents waxed and waned over the course of your life with them, as you developed your own interests, friends, career, and social structure. Yet, your attachment to them created a lasting bond that could not be sundered by separation. Many of you will relate to feeling bonded and should not feel embarrassed by it, despite your age, social, or career accomplishments.

In light of attachment, you can understand the power of losing those upon whom you have depended for much of your life. Those adults who spent a great deal of their adult time with their parents and families have felt emotionally closer or more dependent upon them. These people will relate more to the idea of such a life long attachment. Without understanding the powerful impact attachment has in our relationships, you cannot truly appreciate the power of loss. To understand the nature of attachment, it is important to fully understand the following ideas:

1. Attachment behavior is an instinctive system that results in a person's wanting to attain or keep physical contact with another person.

2. Attachment behavior is separate from and as important as feeding and sexual behavior.

3. Children's attachment behavior leads to the development of affectionate ties later in life.

You begin to appreciate passionately the power of loss when you comprehend the intensity of your parental bonds because of the attachment process. Marsha lost her last parent when she was 43 and had the following to say. "Coming to terms with my parents' deaths meant losing people to whom I was the most attached. I knew they would never be replaced, which made me want to hold on to them more strongly. They will always be an important part of my life."

What is attachment? Attachment is a connection, a bond, a tie. There is nothing closer than a relationship of attachment, and our parental relationships are prime examples. These relationships with friends, lovers, husbands, wives, colleagues are intimate relationships that are important to our lives. When we lose these people, their loss or absence triggers distress that is unique to the loss of that individual and "distress [that] is not to be assuaged by the substitution of another figure in the same relationship (another spouse, another child)."[1]

Matt lost his mother when he was 56. He said, "Nothing affected me like my mother's death. I knew her eventual death would be traumatic, but I was not prepared for the devastation I experienced."

Sydney, who lost her mother when she was 50, put it quite powerfully. "I was prepared for the loss. I was prepared for the ambivalence. But I was not prepared for the heartbreak." Yes. Losing your parents can be heartbreaking.

Relationships of attachment obviously cannot be overestimated in terms of what they mean to us. They affect us deeply, and our need for them is paralleled by nothing else. Yet such relationships can be underrated in importance when considering adult orphans. Rather than perceiving the loss of parents as a minor event for the bereaved adult, it is important to recognize this loss as a life-changing developmental event.

"The death of a parent is not simply a loss. For many adults it is a significant marker event in their life development, one that often promotes intra-psychic and interpersonal changes in the mourner."[2] The loss of a parent is often a loss of a social partner. "For some adult children, parents play an active part in the day-to-day life of their offspring and families. These functions may include being a confidante and adviser on family and marital problems, job-related difficulties, and financial stress. Parents may provide practical assistance, including money, child care, donations of household items, shelter, and other necessities of life."[3] These parents are often relied upon for "grandparent activities," as well as for companionship for their offspring.

Matt, age 38, states, "I know my wife was somewhat surprised at my reaction to Mom's death, she looked at me funny sometimes. I felt it very, very deeply." Obviously, even as adults, you will love your parents a great deal and suffer when they are gone.

Your parents were your most important role models. Although some of you may have felt as though you had "matured" and moved past the need for your parents, others may have felt parental involvement in their lives gave continued support and meaning to their adulthood. It is important to note that the love you have for your parents as an adult is transformed by your understanding of the experience of adulthood. Once you have children, you are likely to understand your parents more fully, and forgive them for their mistakes and limitations. Precisely because we gain respect for the well-meaning parent in adulthood, our love is enriched and our loss is that much greater.

Healthy Families/Healthy Self

Parents and children are vitally important to one another. Together, parents and child create a unit: the family. A healthy family promotes a sense of security, which allows you to develop your own individuality. Many will relate to this and feel lucky to have had parents who supported their own individual growth. Naturally when you grow up in a family, you feel as though your "self" was always apparent. The individual may feel that his or her self was always revealed and have less desire to alter that self after parental loss. Regardless, the adult with a well-identified self, may still benefit from using parental loss as a motivation for creating a still fuller life.

There is the possibility of great love and respect between parents and their children. Despite constantly changing cultural and social factors that can separate generations, it is likely that members of a strongly connected family will achieve the highest quality of life with maturation, personal evolution, and success as reachable goals. This is a wonderful ideal.

It is what you want for your own children—and what you would have wanted for yourself. When you come to appreciate the role of bonding and the behaviors and needs fed by your attachment to your parents, you can understand yourself in relation to your parents in a new way. You will also learn to appreciate the need for and potential for change as an adaptation to their absence.

Generally, good parenting resulted in your having a good sense of self-esteem. Good self-esteem equates to good self-expression. Carole was 58 when orphaned. "I felt my parents wanted me to 'be myself' and they encouraged me to take risks and follow my desires in life. As a consequence I generally felt I expressed myself honestly, whether it was a feeling I was having or whether it was a desire to do something in life."

The "health" of a family or the degree to which family members, children in particular, feel they can "be themselves" varies. Parental influence significantly affects choices and self-expression. The experience of parental loss and the bereavement process signal the beginning of a shift in perspective. After parental loss, you are in a special time of transition, which requires unique adjustments and coping strategies. There is nothing familiar about becoming orphaned.

Your acceptance of the need for adaptation determines your success in your new role as a person without parents. First, you must weather the grieving process, an upheaval that is seldom fully understood. "Mainstream American culture does not easily tolerate strong feelings, particularly those that accompany the despair of profound loss."[4]

When bereaved of both parents, you will find you that have added responsibilities, and that your "safety net" of childhood has been removed. Until now you have depended on your parents in one way or another. They have always been available for everything from nurturance to the possibility of resolving old conflicts with them personally. Their deaths release you from your childhood and the following qualities of childhood:

➤ Lack of power and authority

➤ Lack of being in charge or command

➤ Lack of total self-reliance

Here are typical comments drawn from many individual interviews regarding the new awareness of adulthood when orphaned:

"I finally grew up."

"I didn't realize how much of a kid I still was."

"Can you imagine, I am 62 and still felt like a child? I guess you really never grow up if you still have a parent alive."

"Now that I am the head of the family I feel different as a person. I am in charge."

Loss of the Inner Child

Your adult self is not the only part of you that suffered the loss of your parents. Within you still lives an inner child, and this inner child is terribly disturbed by the death of your parents. It is the child within that continues to yearn for parenting, whatever the age of the adult. This parenting takes many forms: assistance, care, financial support, decision making, nurturance, unconditional love.

Many people feel very much like the child they used to be after the death of a beloved parent and long for the kind of primal mothering or fathering they experienced in childhood. One patient, Zach, age 38, told me that while he was coping with a bout of the flu all he wanted was for his mom to place a damp washcloth on his hot forehead and bring him ginger ale. Zach is a large, burly man, and he was somewhat embarrassed by his deep yearning for maternal love, but such a childlike need for Mom or Dad is very much a part of the grieving process for the newly orphaned adult. In fact, Zach helped assuage his yearnings by spending more time with his own two children and giving them the hugs and love he so much wanted for himself.

The feeling of shame or embarrassment at such a regression is also quite common. For those people who find it hard to let go of the mask of the coping, functional, unaffected adult, the Internet can provide support through chat rooms. Those who visit chat rooms regularly can find an outlet for these emotions with strangers who have the same needs. My patient Felicia, who lost her mother when she was almost 50, found sending e-mails to her best friends a soothing balm and great support. "I kind of wanted to keep a low profile for the first months after she was gone, and I found writing and receiving messages was somehow less invasive than having to talk on the phone. I could be a hermit, and still get comfort and some 'mama love' from my friends." However you express your mourning for the inner child, it must be part of your adjustment to orphanhood. As soon as you release any sense of embarrassment and any preconceptions of how you should grieve for that lost child, you will be able to step fully into your complete adult self and accept your loss.

Sameness versus Change

Despite the fact that you can enjoy the feeling of comfort that comes from the experience of sameness and predictability, the benefits of change and transformation should not be ignored. "Nothing endures but change," according to Heraclitus.[5] Change and the possibility of change occur dramatically after parents die. Keep these ideas in mind as you go through the process:

➤ Change

➤ Release

➤ Take risks

➤ Look for possibilities

Taking risks is described by early grief experts as an indication that grief has ended. Newer theories on grief suggest that change can occur at any point in the grief process. The most productive management of change would be to direct yourself back to yourself at this time in the hope of discovering something new. In *Man's Fate*, Andre Malraux says, "The great mystery is not that we should have been thrown down here at random between the profusion of matter and that of the stars; it is that from our very prison we should draw, from our own selves, images powerful enough to deny our nothingness."[6]

The goal/impulse/instinct to become yourself is present in your psyche, and you can tap into it more easily when parents have died if: your parents had been inhibiting or restrictive or, for your own reasons, you failed to express yourself adequately. Freedom to become yourself is your birthright. If the reason you were less of yourself had to do with seeking parental approval, certainly at the time of their deaths you are no longer enslaved by that pattern.

The following poem was recited to me by a bereaved individual after having a dream about creating a new life goal—that of becoming self-directed and inspired by feeling free.

> *A life, a life created by more than flesh,*
> *Has brought me here now,*
> *My undoing made more real by strokes of dying,*
> *Born upon my newness like a shield.*
> *Oh to know myself now the key*
> *Life's mirror shining toward the light*
> *Fairly, the dark quest over*
> *Ending with my mirth*
>
> —Anon, 2002[7]

Freedom and Liberation

So what is it then that allows the individual to become reoriented around new and self-directed goals? What is responsible for the orphan's beginning the journey toward self-reliance, for taking this opportunity that life now gives? How are you suddenly able to reorganize yourself in a new way?

Feeling freed is one response to a parent's death. This positive feeling often creates a conflict for the survivor, and the reasons are clear. After spending a lifetime bonded to one's parents with love, this feeling of freedom after their deaths creates guilt and other disturbing feelings. These feelings can be shocking and difficult to assimilate.

Many individuals shared their experiences of these conflicted feelings with me:

"I didn't know I would feel free, and I am excited and scared."

"I couldn't identify this feeling of lightness at first, when you said it was freedom, I said, 'Yes!' Then I said 'No.'"

"I knew I was liberated immediately; I felt free and guilty about it."

"When my duties ended, my freedom began."

"I had this thrilling feeling of being able to do anything. But I was afraid to tell anyone because I thought they would think I hadn't really loved my parents."

"My mother told me how free she felt when her own mother died and that I would one day feel the same way! So she ultimately gave me permission to feel it."

"I had to learn to separate out all my feelings after my parents died, but certainly one way I felt was free."

"If only I could have been free when my parents were alive, they might have enjoyed me enjoying my freedom."

It is possible that the internalized parental voices within you will continue long after their lives have ended. You can learn to release these voices and begin to hear your own.

Aloneness Made Positive

Loneliness is very much what you feel as an orphan. It hurts to feel alone. Yet the other side of being alone is there is no one to answer to or to consider (except for your spouse or children). So, in fact, the orphaned state is indeed double-sided— the pain of aloneness is mixed with the joy of freedom. Marty, age 60, a college professor of English, shared many stories with me about what he called his "joy of freedom." Here is one of them:

> One day I was walking to my class and several co-eds came dashing over to me giggling. I noticed my initial reaction, which was one of criticism. Then I said to myself, "I am being like my father, and I don't want to do that." My inheritance left me comfortable, and I made a decision to take a year off. My sabbatical allowed me to visit India for half a year, and the experience made me a more spiritual individual.
>
> I spent the other half of my year in France, studying both art and languages. It was one of the best years of my

life. I had divorced before Dad's death, and I traveled alone. Although I felt lonely sometimes and cut off from all of my familiar roots, I was exploring life on my own and loving it. I met people and enjoyed many good times. In France, I played. I used my senses; I stayed up later than usual. I felt lucky. I promised myself I would return to teaching and help my students understand many things about life:

There are many ways to live life.

There is much to enjoy, and it's good to take time for pleasure.

We must do what we desire and feel passionately about.

When Do You Get to Feel Free?

At what point after the death of your parents do you begin to feel free? It is different for everyone. For some, the sense of liberation was immediate, for others it occurred later in their process. Can you be in conflict over feeling free and still take advantage of the freedom? Yes.

Whether you allow yourself to feel free and accept the changes the freedom prompts depends on your attitude toward freedom. Not all of you will place the same value on freedom. What was your attitude about being free? Remember, many of you will admit to having had feelings of guilt when you first felt free. If you didn't feel guilt, it is also okay. Some felt too guilty to continue and pushed the sense of freedom away.

Separation Begins Again, but Differently

When you are orphaned, the physical separation puts an end to your typical interactions and communications with your parents. This physical separation from parents has emotional and psychological components. As early as the period referred to as the "terrible twos," your need to be "separate" from Mommy began.

During your adolescence your need to separate reoccurred, as your need for individuation expressed itself more strongly. Everyone who has raised a teenager knows the struggle teenagers must endure. When you are orphaned, the process of individuation reemerges. How you respond to the following questions is an indication of where you are.

1. How do you feel about where you are in life? What areas need improvement?

2. How do you feel about your own individual nature? Is it being expressed?

3. If you feel liberated, can you see the benefit of using it for your own benefit?

Research as well as popular nonfiction suggests that there is the potential for a development push after the death of parents. This developmental push can be emotional or psychological. Developmental researchers M. S. Moss and S. Z. Moss say, "This developmental push is concise and informative."[8] It provides the opportunity for you to return to your prior place in your maturational development process and restart where you left off. That is the magic of self-rediscovery.

Margie, age 53, commented, "I didn't realize I was taking up where I had left off. It just felt like I was growing again, growing more consciously than ever before."

For Those Who Feel Guilt

Again, it is not unusual to feel bad about feeling good. Many people reported intense feelings of guilt and remorse about feeling free because they were feeling free at the expense of their loved ones.

"At first I thought it was terrible I felt free, I felt so guilty."

"I felt guilty about moving forward with my own life."

"I felt guilty about becoming self-oriented and self-involved."

"I felt guilty about enjoying life."

"I felt guilty about detaching from my parents."

"I felt guilty about benefiting from my parents' demise."

"I felt guilty about not feeling worse, or not feeling bad longer."

"I felt guilty for adapting."

"I felt guilty for accepting and enjoying a new life style provided by an inheritance from my parent."

"I was afraid I would become totally self possessed."

You feel guilty about growing and becoming the person your parents didn't know. You worry about how your parents would feel about your development, whether they would like you now. It is natural and commonplace to feel some guilt, but do not get stuck.

FIGHTING GUILT

Obviously, the freedom to explore life and to make whatever new choice you desire does not come without anguish. Yet fighting these guilty feelings and moving forward as a free person is possible, and most people can accomplish this goal. To help you understand, ask yourself these questions and write the answers in your journal.

1. Do I live in a culture that acknowledges or values personal freedom?

2. Was I raised in a family that accepted personal freedom?

3. What were my parents' attitudes about freedom?

4. How would I define "freedom"?

5. Were my parents "free"?

6. Were my grandparents "free"?

7. What message about freedom have I given my children?

8. What did my religion teach me about freedom?

Lack of Guilt

I felt:
   energized
   exhilarated
   inspired
   excited about life
   thrilled

These are reactions from people who lost their parents, did not feel guilt, and were free to express their enthusiasm.

> Bess, age 60: "I was tied to my parents and closer to my father than my mother. I was always concerned about my parents' approval. If you had asked either of my parents if I had been freedom loving, they both would have said yes. They also would have told you I had always made my own decisions and did what I wanted to do. They had no idea of the degree to which there was an internal part of myself always monitoring my own desires and many of my impulses."

> Beau, age 58: "My father used to accuse me of never knowing what I wanted to do. I did used to waver between career ideas, and I can understand how I might have made him feel that way. We had such a good relationship; however, he let me wander until I asked for help. He was a good role model for me. Eventually I realized my potential for helping people and became a counselor. I felt free to make this decision. Boy was I in for a shock when my father died. I had always thought of myself as somewhat free spirited, but the surge of freedom that came after his death I could only describe as exhilarating."

> Nancy, age 47:"I was somewhat estranged from both of my parents. I thought one day we would get closer, but that time never came. I moved to the big city after college and never returned home. Did I feel freer after their deaths? Yes. I was not overcome with it, but I did certainly feel a release from childhood."

Release from Childhood

Nancy's comments about the release are important. No matter how free you think yourself to be, when you are no longer anyone's child, you feel even freer. No longer being in relationship to your parents is what frees you. While friendship or spousal liberation also frees you, the liberation from a parental figure is more intense, because of the formative nature of the parent-child attachment relationship.

The loss of a primal relationship of attachment to you is significantly different than any other. You were shaped by the processes of learning and accommodation. The most fundamental task of mourning is to reconstruct a new identity appropriate to the bereaved individual's changed status. In a very real sense, you are no longer who you once were prior to the loss. The possibility of developing a new self or aspects of the self is possible now.

The possibility arises from many factors:

1. The natural instinct to recover from loss.

2. The need to internalize parts of the lost parent to ensure a lasting connection.

3. The need to withstand the loss and prosper.

4. The need to continue living with hope.

5. The need to self-actualize.

6. The need to meet the challenge of loss and grow from it.

Reorganization

It might be helpful to hear what other orphans have said about their experience of parental loss. The following is a list of phrases they used when discussing their changed perceptions:

1. I renewed myself.

2. I was restored.

3. I reclaimed parts of me.

4. I was reborn.

5. I was reorganized.

6. I was uncovered.

7. My truest self was born.

8. I was a different "me."

Orphaned adults want to feel in control of their lives again. They do not necessarily want to return to the way they were before the deaths of their parents, if for no other reason than that they want to change beyond the more limited version of themselves that existed before their parents died. They do not want to be stuck in loss, and they do not want to regress. Orphaned adults naturally become different as a result of the change of roles and power. Psychiatric literature describes the process of mourning resolution as including a return to "normal functioning." At this stage, the idea of normal functioning should include the notion of change and finding out new things about yourself. This is a perfect opportunity to resist the temptation to be "normal," and instead explore what makes you unique.

Adaptation necessarily requires seeking a new solution for a new opportunity. Adaptation is a process of adjustment to new circumstances. So the idea of reorganization rings true. It suggests you will be learning to organize yourself around the new circumstance of having no parents and all that such a circumstance really means.

"The affected individual will recover in the sense that they re-plan their lives and achieve a new independence," says Colin Murray Parkes in *Recovery from Bereavement*.[9] Change is inherent and natural when a parent dies, leaving you to survive on your own.

Coping with loss is a developmental process, according to George Pollack. In his paper "The Mourning Process and Creative Organizational Change," he explains it as being adaptational, "a process by which change, shock, strain and loss are dealt with in order to maintain continuity, integration, cohesion, survival and additional development . . . evolving from a Darwinian process of natural selection which is universal, psycho-social and biological. The outcome is a return to a steady state of balance, even though it is different than the initial one."[10]

> Patricia, age 46: "I was so miserable after losing my parents. Just knowing they existed made me feel secure. I had to do something to survive my shock and loss. So, I changed and became someone who didn't need them anymore. I acknowledged my independence fully for the first time in my life."

Reconnecting to the Birth Self

Reconnecting to the birth self is positive because it acknowledges that the self has always been in existence, though it may have become buried for a variety of reasons. Self-exposure can be threatening, as you become more vulnerable and willing to let others see the real you. But being the "real you" is a sign of psychological health. Being the real you imparts feelings of strength, competence, and wholeness. Your true self may also be vulnerable, unsure, insecure, emotional, and creative.

No Blaming Others Any More

Your orphanhood signals the end of being able to blame anyone but yourself for your own problems. This may be the best way to assure yourself that you are finally becoming an adult. Without anyone else to blame, you must enter adulthood. You now have the opportunity to take full responsibility for everything in your life.

> Mattie, age 56: "My biggest shift was psychological. My loss included my ability to go back to my parents for help, my ability to take advantage of their goodness, and my need to stay immature. I had to do it all for myself, make good decisions, earn a living, and no longer blame anyone. It was difficult but I was committed to these goals."

Describing Self

"As I embrace the new me, I search for an adequate way to describe this process of self-revelation. It is slow and gradual. I sense myself more than think it. I know me when I am quiet and meditative. Yet, me is what I feel inside. I am flexible yet steady. I am adaptable and constant."

"My self is my watering hole to which I turn when I am thirsty."

"My self is something deep within me that directs my actions and thoughts."

"My self has been obscured from vision for so long, I doubt very much I would recognize it. I have played so many roles."

"My self is a concept I have been working on for some time. It is the real me, and I detect it when I ask it this question, 'What do you want?' and then wait for an answer."

Finding the real self at this transitional period of life is the opportunity of a lifetime. Becoming your own best friend or even your own good inner parent is a blessing. This best friend or self-parent encourages you to find greater and greater resources of self.

It is the mature self that can transform grief into growth. This self begins to reexamine life in order to determine what is still important and relevant. As the real priorities of your life emerge, your mature self then begins to eliminate the details that once seemed important, but have diminished meaning in the light of true meaning. It is this self that begins to formulate the essential philosophy that allows you the freedom to accept all of the positive possibilities available to this new or reconstructed self. This is the stage in your life when doors will begin to open seemingly effortlessly, the ambitions you may have kept subdued will begin to warrant exploration, and the goals you have set for yourself will come to fruition. It is the work you have done in moving through grief into a fertile time of growth that makes this possible.

Changes within Relationships

As an orphaned adult you feel alone, so relationships acquire a more significant role in your life. You begin to cherish friendships and people you love so much more. They become your new support systems. In order not to feel alone, you learn to devote more time and energy to friendships and relationships. You may become closer with other family members. There is a tendency and a need to reestablish a sense of family. You might consider seeking out other orphans; they are the best group of individuals with whom to bond, since they are having a similar experience.

After your orphanhood, you may find yourself reaching out to bring your friends much closer to you. The death of parents presents itself as an opportunity to become closer to family members and friends. A study by Andrew Scharlach and Karen Fredriksen in "Reaction to the Death of a Parent During Midlife" indicates that 42 percent of their subjects described closer relationships with friends after losing parents and 35 percent reported closer relationships with family members.[11]

Allowing yourself to accept the changes within your family and social structures reflects your acceptance of your parents' death and your new status. As impossible as it may often feel, your life is now different. Letting others support you is extremely important. Your feelings and needs change and will keep changing over time. Be prepared to adjust to these changes as they occur. Most importantly, trust that these changes will ultimately lead to your growth as an individual.

5

Navigating the Waters: Rediscovering Internal Depths

Regret and doubt are twins that rob us of the day.
—Robert Hastings

N ow is the time to communicate with the deepest part of you. You have been reading about what *can* happen for you. Now is the time to think about what *will happen*. After the initial period of intense grieving for your loss, you will be able to begin to evaluate what has changed in your life.

When you mourn completely, you avail yourself of the total potential that exists for you to rediscover, reclaim, and redesign your life. One way to fully experience the mourning that occurs with the loss of your parents is to keep a journal that traces your path through the grieving process. The record of your journey allows you to become more aware of the ebb and flow of your feelings and the ways in which your emotions impact on your life, particularly in terms of your transformation.

Possible Journal Topics

The process of renewal will take a different form for each individual, but there will be common threads. Here are some pivotal questions to address.

Have you been receiving sufficient support in managing your loss?

If not, have you sought out counseling to help you cope?

Do you find yourself feeling differently? If so, how?

Do you feel that your identity changed?

How have you integrated your loss into your life?

What you are looking for is the connection between the loss of your parents and new beginnings in your life. This new growth and renewal may occur in both your external and your internal life. It will begin with your examination of the aspects of yourself that you may have suppressed during the time your parents were alive. These aspects may now be ready to emerge.

At this point in life, transformation is possible for everyone. Personal transformations take different forms. For example, for someone who remained dependent on his or her parents during adulthood, orphanhood would present an opportunity for independence and self-reliance. Someone who already had an established sense of independence could use adult orphanhood to motivate further creative expansion in work or as an opportunity to build more satisfying personal relationships. An independent adult orphan might also find that this is the time to begin to accept the positive traits he or she has in common with the parent who has been lost. The following examples will clarify this point.

Frances was 49 years old when her last parent died. Frances had always been the "good girl." She did well in school, became a nurse, helped people, and stayed married to an abusive husband for "the kids." When her parents became sick, she became the primary caregiver for the family and did more than her share of the caretaking activities. She did her parents' cooking, took them to their appointments, and was responsible for hiring extra help when needed.

Frances was also very dependent on her parents. She discussed her personal problems with them and often claimed she would rather return to their home than continue to live with her difficult and emotionally volatile husband. She made Sunday night dinners and invited her parents on a regular basis. Her parents babysat for her children and provided emotional support for Frances.

Her husband often complained that Frances was too close to her parents and that closeness had caused problems in their marriage. He used to tell her she had never completely grown up, and blamed her for all of their marital difficulties.

When her parents both died, Frances went through a period of adjustment. One day she made a list of all the things in her life that bothered her, and she decided she would tackle them one by one. Her decision was followed by a period of inactivity. Feeling ambivalent about change is natural. On the top of her list was her personal life: She wanted a divorce. She felt a duty to herself to live a better life, and she needed to live separately from her alcoholic husband. She also wanted a career change and a higher income. Her small inheritance provided her with some economic independence, which would help her make the changes she wanted to make. In addition, her children were getting older and were more capable of sustaining changes their mother might make that would affect their lives.

Maurice was 47 when he lost his last living parent. He had grown up in Michigan and moved to the West Coast after college. He had married a woman he had met soon after his move and had three children. He was from a large family and while he did not return home often, he and his wife and kids would phone on a weekly basis.

When his children graduated high school, he encouraged them to go to college in his hometown to be near his extended family. In many ways, Maurice had been fairly independent of his family. Yet, as he described it, a surprising thing happened to him when he was orphaned. Quite suddenly, he found that he wanted to return to his hometown. He was overwhelmed by a feeling of wanting to go back to his roots.

Before making his decision, Maurice decided to seek counseling. Ultimately, he did take his family back to Michigan, and it was with the intention of being closer to those he loved. For Maurice, achieving further family intimacy began with going home.

The Need for Movement

As the adage has it, "Nature abhors a vacuum." Put another way, in life there has to be movement. The idea of change is threatening to many people, and yet we all know life is filled with changes, large and small. Some change is desirable, such as your children growing up and prospering. Other changes like aging, divorce, moving, and death are considered undesirable. Some of you will view change and growth as a positive occurrence while others of you will not. Some of you will more easily adapt to change than others.

A Life in Motion

After losing parents, individuals make all types of changes and grow in many ways. While some people value growth more than others, almost all of us would agree that a rich life is enhanced by continuous, personal growth.

Possible External Changes

Any physical change to body

A change in environment

A change in home

A change of professional or work setting

A change in living arrangement

A change in who you live with

A change in how you live, for instance, getting up later or earlier

Possible Internal Changes

A change in feeling, emotion, thought

A change in attitude, belief, value, world view

A change of behavior

A change "of heart"

A change in a relationship's importance

A change in view of mortality, life, death

A change in meaning; what's important

A change in religious or spiritual life

Mike was 35 when he was orphaned. Soon afterward, he left his hometown and moved to New York to pursue a business. "I never knew life could be so rewarding. I was comfortable at home, and now look at me. Here I am in a huge city taking new chances in my business and in my life. Sometimes it's a little unnerving, but generally, I feel strong, self-sufficient, and determined to succeed."

Marsha was 46 when orphaned. She died her hair red and became a sex therapist. "Why should I try to be normal anymore, I decided. Normal is boring. I had always wanted to live closer to the edge, but I couldn't do it when my parents were alive, for some reason. I was always trying to fit a certain image I thought they had of me. Now I can be who I want to be."

Matt was 57 when orphaned. He sold all of his possessions, joined the Peace Corps, and went to India. "My spiritual nature was always strong, but I was the oldest son, and my mother lived with me. When she died, I was free to dedicate my life to others, to be the humanitarian I had always thought I could be."

The Ethic of Happiness

There is a process the Greek philosophers called *eudaimonia*, which means human flourishing. In the dictionary, *eudaimonia* is defined as, "happiness, the main universal goal, is derived from a life of activity governed by reason" and "the system of ethics that considers the moral value of actions in terms of their ability to produce personal happiness."[1]

Can you identify with an internal need to flourish? This is a need that is not as apparent as other needs, such as the need for food, shelter, sex, and human contact. Yet, it is a need that is just as important. Though it is not as explicit as the need to have a roof over your head, it is integral to a fulfilled life for the self to maintain integrity through its self-recognition, self-expression, and the realization of positive change. Webster's definition of *flourish* is "to grow vigorously; to succeed; to thrive; to prosper, to be at the peak of development, activity, influence, production; to be at one's prime." The process of flourishing is what naturally occurs at times of great transition in life, for instance, after the birth of children or the death of parents. We all recognize that birth is a joyous occasion, and we often underestimate the power of loss to inspire rebirth. Flourishing and thriving are concepts we tend to reserve for children, but we must realize that we are entitled to flourish and thrive throughout our lives.

Finding Joy

In your journal or on a sheet of paper, answer the following deceptively simple questions as honestly and completely as possible. Then look over your answers in a day or two and see what you can add to your answers.

As you nurture others in your life, do you consider and nurture yourself?

What activities make you feel alive?

What brings you a sense of contentment?

What gives you a sense of satisfaction?

When do you feel happiness?

Do you experience joy?

Do you believe that you deserve to feel good?

Life in this culture demands hard work and effort, so it is easy to forget that deriving pleasure and goodness from life is as essential as hard work. Joy may not be a tangible asset, but it is what makes the day worth living. The sensual aspect of life with its emphasis on what feels pleasurable, what feels "good" is often described as hedonistic and therefore bad, yet it is an essential building block of a balanced and satisfying life. Far from being "bad," the sensual realm provides creativity and inspiration, as well as joy.

Orphanhood is the time to take stock of yourself and your life. Losing your parents in midlife advances the inner stirrings you feel already. The inner stirrings that normally occur at midlife direct you to reevaluate and reassess yourself and what is important to you. Inclinations or traits you once thought were important may fade and others rise in their place.

Your life gives you a myriad of opportunities. As I was told as a young person, life is a table full of glorious foods; take what you want. In later years, certainly in middle age, as you come to reevaluate what matters, you will come to view feeling good as a goal in and of itself.

Rediscovering the Good Things in Life

There is something in me that I value and want to share with the world.

There is something in me I want to see expressed.

There is something in me I need to awaken.

There is something in me that is beautiful and special, and it is just mine.

There is something in me yearning to come out.

I began to want to have fun, and I wanted to laugh. I cherished my own family and particularly my children. I looked in the mirror, into my own face, and said, "I have to live well now."

Time is fleeting, I'd better have some fun. I want to feel good now! I have been so depressed about losing Mom.

How will I ever have fun again? I feel guilty.

I want to do the things I love and am passionate about.

I want a better sex life.

I want to look better.

I want to start all over again.

I want to reach for the stars.

How much time do I have left for good times?

I have only this life . . . which has to be good now.

That's it, no more time to waste!

Whether I knew about it before or not, my need for joy is here now and I respect its right to live and be heard and seen.

Some of you may not have come from positive relationships with parents and may not really know the truths about yourself . . . that you are really okay and deserving of all of life's riches and pleasures. Here are some ways to allow yourself to realize you deserve all the goodness of life.

My Happiness Ethic

To become comfortable with the rightness of change and the true need for happiness, try repeating the following to yourself whenever you are feeling stuck. I call this exercising your *change muscles*.

I am okay.

I am lovable.

I can and want to change.

Change is good.

Changing will make me happier.

Change will bring happiness to my family members.

Change is a natural part of life.

I need to feel happy.

I can and will share my happiness with others.

I need to do what makes me happy.

I need to make others happy.

Happiness is important for my well-being.

The following are the issues you will have to deal with before you can allow yourself to understand that happiness is your right and to begin to set the goals that will help you attain your happiness.

1. I deserve self-expression.

2. I deserve self-love.

3. I deserve more from life.

4. I deserve to get past limitations imposed by my parents.

5. I deserve to set my self free.

6. I deserve to live without blame.

7. I deserve to be "me."

8. I deserve to let go of my parents' voices and find my own.

What's Keeping You from Joy?

Use your journal to write down a list of the seven attitudes that have prevented you from seeking these ideals in the past. (If you have trouble writing down seven impediments all at once, try keeping notes during the day, when you come face-to-face with an attitude that is holding you back.)

Choosing Freedom in the Wake of Negativity

Finding your innate freedom requires that you understand that freedom is of value. You may need to rid yourself of an internal voice that says "No," or "I'm afraid." Sam, who was 40 when his father died, is a good example of what can happen to someone with an extremely critical father. Here is his story.

> What I remember most about my father was his authoritative quality. Dad was always "right." I never felt that there was room for me to make a statement about myself or my belief . . . somehow Dad would shut me out. He was so set in his own ways. He was also critical about everything in life, including his children. I always thought he should cut us some slack, but no, he never did. He had a method for everything and his way was always the right way.
>
> So, now that he is deceased, how am I supposed to just snap into being and feeling different? I am a product of his environment. . . . I have internalized many of his attitudes and ways of being. I feel lousy about myself. I don't feel motivated to change. I don't even know if it is possible. I just want to go about my life how I am comfortable. It seems like walking on hot coals to think about changing. I just don't think about it.

Sam is stuck in bad feelings. He has accepted the way his father treated him as gospel and has become his own negative critic, judge, and jury. Sam is locked into seeing himself one way and may never change, most particularly because he believes it is impossible.

Roberta, age 47, has a similar story. She is someone with a variety of interests and talents, but no aspirations. She had settled for living a small life and didn't want to hear about possibility. Roberta's father died when she was young, and she grew up with her mother, who suffered from depression. Their life was neither rich nor full. Her mother barely made a living, and they struggled to get along. Roberta left home as soon as she graduated from high school and went to work as a secretary.

She described her marriage the same way she described her life: "ordinary." When her mother died, "It was no big deal." "I was always independent, so not much changed." When asked to examine her inner life, Roberta just smiled and asked, "Do I have one?"

Roberta has an inner life, but she has chosen to bury it. Your inner life is there, but you must respond to it. Your inner life depends upon you to nurture it. You must respond to it, develop it, manage it, and feed it as if it were your internal garden. As Voltaire's Candide so knowingly expressed it, "We must cultivate our garden." Each of us is responsible for our own inner growth. A cultivated inner life produces the most wonderful results, but it takes time to attune yourself to what motivates and nurtures your own individual inner life.

Fortunately, most of you are not like Roberta. The more you ask for and work for, the more you will receive. Each of us does have an internal critic, but unlike Roberta, most of us find the determination and courage to face up to this critical inner voice. For some, this critic is active in many parts of life and spends a great deal of time expressing itself. For others, the internal critic is quieted by a conscious effort to keep it at bay. Often, the critic is the replica of one of your parents, and, in some cases, both. The internal judge is a similar energy and has an effect on your behavior similar to your parents' criticisms and demands. Most of you will agree, the behavioral consequence of the critic or judge tends to be inaction.

> Maxine, age 52: "My mother used to say, 'No, you can't do that,' when I would become too excited about a new adventure. She wanted to keep me quiet, safe, practical, and reasonable. She was not a risk taker herself, and she felt threatened by having to deal with a daughter who was."

> Bruce, age 54: "My father was critical. I never knew if I was smart or not. He didn't give me any positive reinforcement, and I felt he didn't think I would ever make anything out of myself."

> Pam, age 50: "I always felt criticized. No matter how much they loved me, I still felt they were critical of me. Now, I still carry all that criticism with me, and it can be debilitating. I am surprised I can function at all."

Your Critical Voice

Take this opportunity to answer the following questions in your journal.

Can you identify your parents' critical voice?

Did your parents' critical voice become your own?

Can you identify your own voice?

Can you separate your own voice from your parents' critical voice?

The critical part of you is apt to appear many times during your orphanhood, because as you approach the discovery of your freedom you will absolutely run into the obstacles of guilt, fear, blocking, resistance, and self-criticism. It is important during this process of self-discovery to stay open, to allow feelings of opposition to appear, and then to let them go while you continue to stay open to change and feelings of expansion.

The Duality of Movement

As you move toward your goal, you may feel conflict. It is a struggle to make positive changes and choices in life when your independent thinking is being hampered by a critical inner voice. As this occurs, you will notice you are moving away from your goal. This is an aspect of normal progress. There are always two sides to growth, one is action toward the goal and the other is action away from the goal. This pattern is followed by another action toward the goal, and so on. Don't be surprised, discouraged, or taken aback by what looks like inaction; it is not. This is just part of the cycle in the duality of movement back and movement forward.

Grant was 48 when orphaned. He spoke eloquently about this duality of movement:

At first I was so confused by what looked like a total block to my progress. I had worked for months on myself to get ready to make changes in my life. I had decided to look for another job after my father's death. I had inherited some money which allowed me to quit work, and my brothers, who both were employed by his company, decided to buy me out.

I was free to do anything I wanted. I had never really felt working with my family was right for me. I wanted to be a therapist. I requested tons of information from several schools and then, when it all arrived, I did nothing with it for weeks. I wondered about my inertia. I discussed it with my wife who said I may not really have wanted to go to graduate school, but I knew in my gut I did. I continued to be inactive. I questioned whether part of my block had to do with guilt feelings about leaving the family business or just plain fear about my ability to make it on my own. I just felt resistance.

It was a big step for me. When I could, I gathered strength and continued on my new path, I filled out the forms and sent them back. That was the biggest block I experienced. Later my feelings of doubt surfaced, but were easier to manage and never stopped my activity for such a long period of time. It had taken months to gather my courage before sending in my application, finally I did.

Grant was able to navigate the duality of movement and eventually make the changes in his life he wanted to make because he refused to give in to the regressive part of the duality. The people I describe next have not been that lucky, at least not yet.

This resistance to forward movement almost paralyzed Maureen, who was 58 when she lost her last parent. "I always promised myself that when I could, when my kids were out of college and my parents were gone, I would finally start thinking about myself. I told myself I would lose weight, start dressing better, and care more about how I looked. That didn't happen. For some reason, after Mom died, I gained weight . . . lots of weight. It was so strange, because it was exactly the opposite of what I thought I wanted. It has been a year now, and I am still fatter than ever."

Ron, a 44-year-old who lost his mother when he was 15 and his father when he was 37, became totally immobilized after the death of his dad. He stopped discussing his father. He went to the funeral, but wouldn't visit his dad's grave. Ron developed a very common pattern of dealing with grief. He simply refused to deal with it. Instead, he suppressed his grief and lost out on the opportunity for movement and growth. Ron stayed stuck where he was.

You can look within yourself and make strides in your personal growth or you can choose not to do that. It is a choice everyone has to make. There are many individuals who choose not to examine themselves deeply and, therefore, miss out on taking advantage of this fertile period. There is no right or wrong way to grieve; yet the manner of grieving carries with it a consequence. Those who do not choose to look within and move forward in a new direction may find that one consequence is boredom or even depression. Those who embrace the challenge to lead the examined life will reap many rewards and find that they are living a life filled with possibilities and fulfilled potential.

Risk Taking

Risk takers are considered courageous. Risk taking is not something everyone is comfortable with. The loss of your parents changes your identity in the world. It would seem logical that this would be the scariest time to make changes. The main point of this book and the positive paradox of adult orphanhood is that this is actually one of the most fruitful and exciting times in life. Some individuals, with whom I spoke either in interviews or in therapy sessions, have expressed the following sentiments about taking risks. They are important to share:

> "I never thought I could accomplish what I have, I feel so good about my new way of being in the world."

"It's too bad I couldn't have been their child and an orphan at the same time, my life now is so rich."

"I couldn't have made the changes without the support of my husband/wife and children."

"There were plenty of times I doubted my own ability, but I took chances and they all worked out in my favor."

"I would encourage my friends to make changes and to risk whatever they had to!"

"The cost of losing my parents was very high, but the benefits of taking risks and meeting new goals were an unexpected treasure."

"Parental loss is bittersweet, you lose your past and you gain your future."

Who Is This Authentic You?

In Chapter 3, I discussed the birth self, a conglomerate of needs, inclinations, energy systems, personality traits, and potential. The birth self is also a source of motivation, inspiration, and incentive.

You may think of your earliest self as the most authentic part of you. Many people feel their earliest self is their "soul," something they are born with that communicates who they really are. The following examples show the variation among people's views as they attempt to explain in words the inner layer called self.

"Inside I feel something which governs everything."

"When I am quiet, I sense what I call a core."

"I don't remember when I starting attending to my inner voice, but when I did, I felt more honest."

"I have a center which speaks to me when I close my eyes and focus on it."

"I commune with what I call 'me.'"

"It is myself."

"It's like my heartbeat, a drum."

"My self is my heart, my soul, my being, I cannot see it, it's there to be experienced and listened to."

"My self is an awareness."

"My deepest sense of self is a consciousness."

Your Inner Self

In your journal, write the honest answers to the following questions.

Who is your birth self?

Did your parents know that part of you?

Did you try to share your birth self or aspects of it, and what was the result?

What would you say to your parents now about your birth self?

Are there parts of your birth self you wish you could have expressed sooner?

Do you have any regrets?

Discussions of "real selves" can sometimes make people feel uncomfortable, as though they have been living a lie all of their lives. It has not been a lie. You know how easy it is to hide, to cover, to shrink, to become lost in the need for approval or the need to please another person. All of you have subjugated your real self at some time in the service of satisfying a need or goal for yourself or another. It is natural to become fearful of expressing some aspects of your real self. However, to continue to live this way is not necessary. It is time to gain more access to your natural essence. It is your responsibility to release any part of you that had been caged.

These are the key factors about the real self:

➤ The real self is often hidden or kept guarded beneath other selves you create in order to function effectively in the larger world.

➤ The real self is capable of constant change, growth, and adaptation.

➤ The real self is vulnerable to influence by significant others in your life.

➤ You are most satisfied and more effective when you are functioning from within your real self and least satisfied and less effective when you are functioning from within your inauthentic selves.

Share the feelings that were expressed by others like yourself:

Robert, age 56: "After losing my parents, I understood how to become more myself. Even so, intellectually, it required a lot of work. I saw that I could push my parents' visions away and let mine come out, but it took a lot of work to accomplish this and it was easier to ignore it all. I am currently stuck in all of this mess!"

Mike, age 45: "I noticed how fearful I had been and that my fear was wrapped up in my need for parental approval. This discovery allowed me to really look at my own intention to stay safe within boundaries set by someone other than myself. The work involved becoming clear about what I wanted to release and then letting myself do it."

Mary, age 40: "I had always been someone concerned with other people's needs and feelings and I was anxious to begin thinking about myself. No more being such a 'good girl.' I was selfish and impulsive I must admit, at least for a while, but I calmed down after a year. I finally learned to channel my enthusiasm for my newfound freedom into something useful and I founded a homeless shelter for battered women in my town. I was not an abused or battered woman, but I had always had an affinity for the underdog. This was an interest my father tried to discourage, but in his absence I felt free to do what I wanted."

Sam, age 56: "I know my wife has encouraged me to take chances now that we are certainly more financially comfortable than ever, but I am still overly cautious. Just because my parents are gone doesn't give me freedom to do whatever I want. Something, maybe . . . something within reason, but I don't know what that is yet. So, I wait and think about it. One day I will move on it!"

Following Your Path

Change and transformation do not occur with the snap of the fingers. Although there can be an immediate psychological and emotional shift because you are no longer the child of your parents, there is a series of issues and demands that will eventually require coping and the development of new skills. It may take some time to become comfortable with this new state of mind. The added responsibilities of your life require diligent and dedicated work.

For example, anyone who relied on their parents for financial planning will agree that it was quite an adjustment to take over their own financial responsibilities:

Matt, age 39, remarked: "When my parents died, I inherited cash, bonds, stock, and property. My parents had relied on the advice of a man I didn't really like. I had no idea about how to handle so much property; I avoided it all for months. Finally, I had to make a decision about what to do.

"My father had a large manufacturing company and after my divorce I went to work with him. After his death, I was the natural person to take over and that is what I did. I enjoyed business and had watched his skills over the years and learned all I could from him. I didn't resent being there after he was gone. The company prospered in his absence, and I was happy for the opportunity to take on more of his role."

Samantha, age 61, had this to say: "It was easy for me. Now that I am orphaned I have no one to fall back on, I realize, but I am old enough finally to completely grow up. I am a rational person, and I know there is no reason to dwell on feeling any other way."

Natural Changes

Once you begin to adjust to the loss of your parents and accept that you need not feel guilt once you begin to experience growth after their deaths, you will begin to see that this emergence of self-aware-ness is natural and meant to be. Here are some of the important nat-ural changes that may occur:

The natural shift of power

Taking over for the parents in decision making

Becoming head of the family

The necessary evolution of self-reliance

The developing feeling of self-sufficiency

Continuing opportunities for additional responsibilities over time

Continuing personality and psychological changes

Perhaps you need to seek help or comfort from others. Friends and spouses are terribly important now. You need people with whom to share your feelings. You need someone to listen to you. Others in your situation are great sounding boards. This is a time of crisis and requires the same treatment as all other crises: talking with others, understanding, and patience.

My hope is that you find an awakening of a new consciousness, the consciousness of true adulthood. You become a biological adult when you reach maturity, sexuality awakens and you take responsibility for yourself. But there is a quality of adulthood you cannot actually achieve while you are still someone's child. The death of your parents in effect launches you toward this event. All of your awareness changes as you adapt to a world without parents. Your awareness of illness, death, and life changes when you are marked by so powerful an event as the loss of your parents.

Pat, age 50, expressed her experience as follows:

> One of my most vivid memories of this experience was the day I went to see my parents' attorney to sign papers releasing funds for my brother and me. Usually I wear jeans and a shirt to work; I am in the design business and my clothing needs to be comfortable. However, that day a funny thought ran through my head, "I am going to be inheriting a great deal of money and property, and I had better look like an adult." I hadn't ever felt that way before, and, believe me, I spent my share of time in corporate meetings.
>
> I realized I needed to change as a result of adapting to the loss of my parents. Although I had sometimes taken my parents' feelings for granted, I had always known they would be there for me. When they died, I wanted to regress, but I had to become strong.

You may be surprised by the amount of courage you are able to demonstrate after losing your parents. It will surprise you to see how well you perform and cope with your new challenge. Janine, age 43, commented: "I wish I could have developed before the deaths of my parents, I would have liked myself more and accomplished what I wanted sooner."

Childish ways can still dominate your adult life. Regression into behaviors unbecoming of adults is common. You all know this to be true. It is generally a relief to finally grow up and put immature behaviors behind you. When parents die, you lose the feeling that you are the center of someone's life (which can enhance your narcissism). This is a moment of great *loss* and great *gain.*

Sandy, who had lost her last parent when she was 51, told me this in one of our sessions: "Even though I wanted to call out to Mom or Dad to come back, to reverse the irreversible, not to be left yearning for mommy and daddy, I had to grow up. I will release myself from the minor role of kid and pass into the role of adult." The sadness over losing parents continues throughout your lifetime, but adjustments and adaptations are made. Shifting roles account for much of what changes in regard to power and authority. Giving yourself permission to grow, to become self-aware, to engage lost aspects of yourself continues the process. One patient cleverly stated the demand she made for herself to grow like this, "Self, front and center!"

Getting Started on the Way

Most of the people I interviewed for this book shared the experience of having support for their growth. Support came from therapists, family, spouses, children, and friends. Permission for life comes from you now. Things are not always easy, but there is strength in every new day and new meaning in your life. As a child, you waited for someone to give direction, make a demand, create an environment of expectation, or set your goals along with you. It is now up to you to take responsibility for all of these things.

Watching Yourself

One technique that will help you get started on the path to rediscovering your internal depths and building your new outlook is "self-observation." Watching for new behaviors, impulses, ideas, and inclinations generally results in success. New actions must be rewarded and reinforced. Often you will experience a change as a reminder, "I always knew I was good at this, I don't know how I forgot about it." Here are some examples of successful self-observation:

"Losing touch with dance was losing part of my soul. I loved it as a kid, if I had stayed with it . . . who knows what might have happened. But, I let it go and that seemed to be okay with my parents."

"With my own children, I encouraged them to perform their talents as much as possible, even if it was not to be their career. My parents treated me differently."

"I can remember acting a certain way when I was young, then something happened and I changed. . . . Now I want to recover that me."

"One day I woke up and I just felt like putting on more makeup . . . like my mother did. That was new for me."

"My sister told me I was getting really funny, I thought I had always been funny but perhaps I held in my sense of humor, I must have gotten the message from someone to be serious."

"My wife told me after my father died, that I developed his weird sense of wit. I thought I always had some, but I did begin to emulate him more; it was unconscious."

"I loved being in charge, and after my parents died, I loved it more. I was always called a control freak, then I noticed I moved into the position of tyrant!"

"After my father died, I sat down at my children's piano and began to play a short tune. . . . I had liked music but never thought I had talent. Obviously I did have some interest."

"One day I got to my office, looked around, and felt this awful sense of nausea. I stood up and decided to quit! Just like that!"

"After I began to feel more comfortable with my new freedom, I decided to explore all my old passions: animals, dance, and music!"

"I had dreams, oh such wonderful dreams. What happened to them? Now may be the time to return to these old dreams."

Your birth self will reveal itself in flashes of thought, intuition, visions, pieces of daydreams, attractions to other people or activities, your own dreams, and memories from your past. Or, it is possible you are extremely aware of what you want to do or how you could be different. If, for example, you have suppressed being or acting a certain way because of any form of perceived parental limitation, those behaviors are under the surface waiting to spring forth.

Here are some examples:

Martha, age 53, said, "I knew my parents didn't like it when I was angry with them so I had to suppress my feelings. Often, I would become hostile, which they disliked even more. I used to develop headaches from all my unexpressed tension. But, I was resolved not to yell at them.

"Of course this pattern persisted into other relationships and, after their deaths, I had to learn to express myself more quickly and directly when I was mad about something. My husband and my children benefited the most from my change in pattern."

Patty, age 61, remarked, "Like so many of my generation, I suppressed my creative side. I became a teacher but really would have liked to have been an artist. My personality was that of an artistic person, which I also think threatened my parents. So, when they died, not only did I return to art, but I allowed my artistic nature to flourish. That inspired me to look different, attend different kinds of functions and social events, and think and feel more sensually about life in general.

"It was easy to reconnect to my 'inner artist.' I said okay to her and she popped right out! She communicated to me through desire. I knew what she wanted to wear, how she wanted to speak to people; she was much more spontaneous than the good girl within me, and she liked to talk to people about intellectual ideas. She wanted to go to clubs and art shows and wear black. Would it have been so terrible to let her out more of the time when my parents were alive? Probably not! Did I do it? No."

Jim, age 39, said, "My dreams are very colorful, interesting, and informative and that is how I first came to see my inner self. I had a dream that I was on a trek in Pakistan. I was wearing long robes and my head was covered with a pale blue turban. I was with many other people and felt excited.

"When I woke up and thought about my dream, I remembered something from my youth. I had seen a movie about an explorer and had been fascinated by the idea of adventure. I had never, myself, had an adventure, I hadn't even traveled much. I understood my dream to suggest to me I might deeply enjoy both such activities. I bought a magazine on traveling and felt excitement as I read it. Yes, I wanted to explore some other land or continent, and reconnecting to those ideas made me feel really good."

Catherine, age 58, said, "I had a dream after my mother died. I turned to her in the backseat and looked her directly in the eyes. I asked her why she had never wanted me to be a dancer. . . . She blamed it on my father: 'He didn't want you to. It wasn't what he saw for your life.'

"Days later, I gave birth to my dancer again, many years later, and perhaps many years too late, but there she was. I let her take over and she picked classes to attend, and she filled my body with her spirit. I haven't lost contact with her to this day, even as you see, I am not on stage performing. Yet, I dance with her and keep her fed."

If nothing seems different at first, don't become impatient. The process of moving from grief to recovery of self takes time. Change might take you completely by surprise, or you might have been watching and waiting. The idea of recovering the birth self suggests that the birth self has been a wonderful constant in your life. That is what you really have to fall back on.

Berta, age 43, said, "I derived great satisfaction and relief when I realized that I had myself to depend on after my parents were gone. I felt so much stronger and knew that whoever I had been, I had always been, and it was good for my self-esteem. I guess I wasn't so bad! All those years of personal insecurity and feelings of inferiority seemed to disappear as I began to use all of myself. I filled out."

Maxine, age 51, commented, "When my best friend's parents died, I saw her change and become so much more efficient and bold. I talked to her about it, but it never clicked until my own parents died. What a difference it makes to be on your own in life. Makes you feel like you really always had a purpose and now there is no more time to waste."

To flourish as the hero or heroine of your own life requires a commitment to reclaim your lost passions. You may have thought that your passions were dreams of little importance. As you mature, you realize that it is your passions which express something special about your own inner nature.

The journey that you embark upon when you become an orphan is exciting, powerful, and ripe with promise. Both the journey and the destination will bring you untold joy and a passion for living in your remaining years. On this journey you can be anyone you choose to be and do anything that inspires your dreams and aspirations. You can forgive your parents their transgressions, their weaknesses, the ways in which they failed to meet your needs or be the people you wanted them to be. Once you no longer pour your energies into the disappointment, frustration, resentment, or even rage that can result from living without experiencing forgiveness for others' frailties or failures, anything is possible. You can let go of the internal and external boundaries that limit you and instead redesign your life from the ground up.

6

The Hero Within

There is hope in men, not in society, not in systems, not in organized religious systems, but in you and in me.

—J. Krishnamurti, The First and Last Freedom

You find your inner hero as you adapt to the change that is inherent in the transformation from childhood/adulthood to orphanhood. There is no other way to describe it. It can only be the hero who takes up the challenge and embodies the courage to take risks. Obviously, spending many years, even the years you have been an adult, suppressing parts of your personality and your being has taken a toll on you. As a result, it has probably become a way of life that is natural and feels normal for you, and anything that means changing your way of being in the world is going to feel risky.

The drive to reclaim your essence is the fuel powering your journey in new directions. As you move toward destinations that are in some ways unknown, yet in other ways deeply familiar, you move away from adaptation and toward transformation. This journey is highly unique, deeply moving, and potentially life altering. However, instead of becoming someone new, what this transformation offers you is the powerful opportunity to *re*-become yourself.

As natural as change is, it involves risk taking. This puts you into the kind of threatening situations that always arise when you take chances. Although orphanhood does not necessarily produce risk takers, or result in the modification of personality traits in total, it certainly offers you the opportunity to develop those aspects of yourself that will balance out your preconceived notions of how to approach life.

While those with whom I have worked have not "thrown all caution to the wind," they have slowly and methodically made new choices that they describe as "small risks, taken one at a time." The most common statement about change was this: "Over time, I could see myself making changes; some were dramatic and others were subtle."

As you adapt to the change from childhood/adulthood to orphanhood, you will begin to tap into your inner hero. We think of a hero as one who is capable of great deeds and achievements and is brave enough to overcome all obstacles in the way to a valued goal. The word *hero* derives from the Greek, "to watch over, to protect." So, the inner hero is also there to watch over you and see to your welfare as well as to serve as your source of courage and inspiration.

The inner hero is one of your strongest assets in using your loss to change your life. Heroism incorporates your inner explorer and adventurer. The hero is a warrior with endless energy and the courage to complete the identified task; your hero is your risk taker and your guide. In literature and mythology, the hero is an innocent in need of growth, maturation, and development. The hero loses innocence and gains knowledge after the trials and tribulations of a personal journey. The journey is complete when the hero has become transformed in some way and returns home renewed and permanently changed. This completed journey suggests that the hero has accomplished an important quest, the results of which include personal development and maturity.

Your Inner Hero

Here are some perceptions of who your inner hero might be:

The part of me that is the strongest

The part of me that is courageous

The me who takes action quickly

The part of me that I have come to know recently, which seemed to arise out of my fear of death and worry about how I could cope with no parents left

The one inside who sees the biggest picture

The part of me that has no feeling of fear or insecurity

The part of me that likes challenge

The part of me which is physical and mental more than emotional

The me who is the problem solver

The me who is the leader of the pack

When asked how they felt as children about their parents dying, most of the people with whom I shared information said that the death of their parents had been too painful to think about. Some thought it would be an impossible event to cope with. When they thought about it, they would automatically shut off and think about something else. They were not capable of dealing with it before it happened. Some thought that they would be fine when the time came. Yet for many it remained in the back of their minds as something horrible they would one day have to deal with. They hoped they would be stronger at that time. It is possible that we all carry the awareness of future parental death somewhere in our psyches. We know that one day we will be called on to live without our parents. It has been called "anticipatory grief." Once you had faced the challenge of coming to terms with parental death, the feelings of accomplishment were great. "This process, as difficult and rewarding as it can be, creates the space for 're-ordering priorities and appreciating the richness of life.'"[1]

Comments like, "I never knew I was so strong," "I have now tested myself in a new arena and passed," or "If I hadn't found my inner strength, the most heroic part of me, I would never have been able to cope with my life after Mom and Dad died" were commonplace.

Reclaiming the parts of your self that have been lying dormant for so many years is a major theme in this book. Finding strength you never knew you had is the gift of parental death. In strength there is ability, and in ability there is motivation. What most of the subjects with whom I have spent time have revealed is this: Not only did I grow into adulthood, but I found a link to my passions and my lost dreams.

The Return to Self

A return to one's passions and dreams is illustrated by the comments below:

"I regrouped and changed my priorities, which included doing the things I had always been passionate about."

"I never dreamed my life would change so much after my parents died; I was really shocked. I felt so different."

"Feeling different didn't come all at once. It came in stages and over time."

"I had dreamed about being an actress, but never thought I had the talent. Now, I jump into any activity that resembles acting with joy."

"I had a lifetime dream, to own a horse farm. . . . Well now I have one. Every day of my life now I am doing what I love."

"My dream was always to be involved with helping old people. When Dad was sick and I was at the hospice on a daily basis, I learned about what the dying need. Now I have volunteered at the same facility and, despite my memories, I am involved in helping others."

"I never believed in my dreams. Now I make myself take risks. I am working on rediscovering what my dreams were, and I will follow them . . . I promise!"

"I always told my kids to follow their dreams, which is unusual because I never learned that lesson in my own home. I always did what I thought I should do, but now that my parents are gone, my own children have been encouraging me to listen to my own words . . . so I am working on it. I am recovering my lost dreams. I do remember I was passionate about art and sailboats."

"I started living life my way . . . doing what I loved."

There were, doubtless, ideas, hobbies, people, situations, places, or talents you were passionate about once in your lifetime that you may have put aside. You need to remember what these passions were. When asked directly about this, many people acknowledged that they felt they had not been encouraged to pursue their own interests in certain parts of their lives. When asked, "Are you doing what you love in life?" Most people answered "No."

There is no better time to gain access to things you have been passionate about than when you are orphaned. You are motivated by your sense of mortality. You have time and space because your children may be out of the house and your parental caregiving role is over. It is time for you.

Many of the people I interviewed admitted that their parents did not like or accept what they were passionate about. The parent or parents "in power" felt their child's goal to be either impractical or unacceptable for some reason. Some of these people said that their ambitions threatened their parents, and that a personal goal seemed to remind the parents about themselves and some of their own unsatisfied ambitions.

True, children do not have to listen to their parents' restrictions or attitudes, and some of them do not. Yet, there are large numbers of people who did. Many people would say, "I agreed with my parents' idea about what they wanted me to do in life, and I think they were right." Practicality and the need for security and survival played important roles in the decision to let go of passions.

For example, Lani, age 57, was very good at playing the piano. Lani's mother had been a musician herself and was unhappy about her own lack of success. Despite Lani's talent and passion for music, her mother discouraged her from pursuing a musical career. Lani, who always sought her parents' approval, listened to her mother and early in her life gave up her dream of a career as a concert pianist. Instead, she chose to educate others about music.

Tory is another example of someone who abandoned his passion. Tory was 51 when his last parent died. He had wanted to be an actor, but this was never acceptable to his family. So he told himself he wasn't handsome enough or good enough, and he abandoned this goal. Many years later, Tory recognized his personal loss of self-expression.

Where do you look if you want to find parts of yourself you have abandoned? Needless to say, it is an inner search. In addition to going back into your life to rediscover an abandoned passion, you might decide to discover something completely new. For example, Mark had always wanted to paint, but he decided to be practical and become a physician in order to ensure that he could make a living. At age 58, after the deaths of both parents, he felt a lack of satisfaction so he decided to paint again. In addition, and seemingly out of nowhere, he decided to take up bicycle riding. In a very short time, riding his bike became a great passion. He had found great pleasure in something completely new.

The process of searching the self for old passions or to discover new ones requires fortitude and commitment; strengths you didn't know you had. Why does this strength seem suddenly to appear from nowhere? According to Thomas Moore, in *Care of the Soul*,[2] it is during times of grave crisis that the *soul* appears and gets you through what otherwise would have been an impossible situation. In other words, resources not previously experienced make themselves available for managing the crisis.

This is the opportunity I want to help you claim. After you lose your parents, you are given the opportunity to transform into the *you* you were intended to be from the beginning of your life, and it is your inner hero that will help you navigate to the true you.

No More Parental Restriction: Recovering Creativity

It is important to reclaim your creative impulse. Whether you sing or act or draw or write, it is necessary to reconnect to the part of you that contains the potential for creative enterprise. Connection to this aspect of your self releases your vitality for living, change, and growth—for appreciating loved ones, enjoying an evening of theater, loving your work, or enjoying the preparation of a special meal. When you activate your creative side, you assure yourself there will be change and forward movement.

Without the ability to contact your creative or instinctive side you are left without a critical part of your own nature. This aspect of your nature is what helps you make good decisions. It is the part of you that knows what is right for you to do and helps you achieve a well-balanced equilibrium between your rational and emotional responses to life.

Were You Fearful of Negative Parental Reaction?

Fear of negative reactions like disapproval or something even worse can rob you of your passions. "The things I was passionate about were just not okay!" say many with whom I have worked or spoken. "The negative message wasn't necessarily overt, but I knew it was there anyway." said Marsha, age 67, years after her parents' deaths. "My parents were very clear about what they wanted in the family and it had nothing to do with what I wanted!"

Of course, the first step is to release any of your own internal restrictions: the voice that says, "You can't do it now, it's too late," or "What makes you think you can do it now?" or "Your parents were right, and they still are." Unless you become immobilized by your own inner sense of limitation, now you can go for broke. You can do anything you want. You can be and do whatever you wanted. Remember your passions!

Lisa, age 49, lost her entire creative instinct: "I was always such a creative person, I loved to draw, and paint, make things. . . . I gave it all up to become an accountant, because that is what my father wanted me to do!"

Michael, age 57, said, "I loved music. It was my life. I played the piano and took lessons for years. I wanted to learn to play the drums and the violin and the harp, but my parents laughed and said, 'Just play the piano and play it well.' How do I know what might have come from one of the other instruments. . . . We will never know."

As Henry David Thoreau observed, "The mass of men lead lives of quiet desperation." How true. Such an observation may lead us to ask: "So now that we know that, what happens next? Pick up and fight? Does it matter? Can anything be done at this age?" You can do it for yourself, when you let the inner hero be your coach.

The Voices of Being a Hero to Yourself

You can do this!

Now it's your time!

It's never too late!

Take the risk!

It is hard to clear away the cobwebs of the past. Who you are has to do with everything that is still in your head from childhood. These teachings stay with you and manifest themselves as moods, beliefs, and memories. When you clear these lessons of childhood away and begin to see yourself without the shadow of your parents, positive changes will and do occur.

A healthy home life instills in all of us the willingness to try new things. As children, it is hoped that you were encouraged to follow your assertive and aggressive impulses, particularly as they applied to your becoming more autonomous and self-regulating, with inner freedom and vitality. There is a new vitality of life that ignites after the death of parents and the experience of loss. Springing back with vitality is the step that can be taken away from death and feelings of loss and deprivation. To function and to function well again, albeit to function differently, is your new goal. Indeed, this is the goal for anyone who wants to live a fulfilling life.

Healing Wounds from the Past

The process of self-reparation, or the restoration of lost aspects of the self, has many positive attributes. Repairing the self by reconnecting to disowned or unrealized parts of the self is what I am calling self-reparation here. The first and most obvious reward is reclaiming the energies that have been lost. A second reward is the subsequent increase in self-esteem as you internalize feelings of strength, courage, and power that are descendants of the heroic act of self-illumination.

Healing occurs when you reclaim lost parts of yourself. It is hurtful to the self and the sense of self to live without all of the self's vital aspects. This absence of vital parts, whether you are aware of it or not, plays a role in your overall self-experience. The loss of vital parts registers deep within the psyche, affecting your mood, your personality, and your sense of accomplishment. Readjusting the self through reconnection restores the unity, integrity, and wholeness of your center or self, that part of you that makes you who you are.

One of my friends and teachers, Dr. Hal Stone, called our personal centers "the essence of what makes us ourselves." I concur. Using the term *essence* is a notable way of describing the internal nature of individuals. If the very essence of who you are as an individual is not appreciated and directed to express itself by your will or intention, serious wounding occurs. This wounding is manifested in such symptoms as boredom, restlessness, depression, feelings of emptiness, angst, personal dissatisfaction, and lack of creativity.

When there is no creative force working for the self, the self and passion wither. The individual feels unhappy and his or her personality and relationships suffer. Everything is not lost, however. All can be restored and the time for that restoration is now. In the absence of parental expectation, or your own need to please, the previously unacknowledged parts of your essence can be restored and resurrected. In so doing, healing occurs and a new life is born. It is the renewal of the life force that can bring you back to yourself as you begin again to develop and to become. That is why I have said, *"Parents give birth to us twice, once when we are born and once when they die."*

Deficit Selfhood

The "deficit selfhood" is the self before it is renewed. It lacks many of its most vital aspects. These missing aspects are passions, talents, inclinations, or perceived positive traits.

Here are some examples of deficit selfhood shared with me over the years:

> "I always knew I could be practical, but my mother's constant criticism pushed me into becoming someone who would act rebelliously rather than conform."

> "My brothers and sisters all went to college; I refused because I thought it would please my parents if I went to work as soon as I graduated high school. I thought that perhaps they needed my income. I never examined any of my talents. I knew I had to be good at something; I just never explored what that might be . . . until they both died."

> "My father wanted me to be a dentist. His father was a dentist, and my older brother was a dentist. I naturally became one too. Was it right for me? I never even thought about it. . . . I just followed suit."

> "I have never stopped being angry with my father for not encouraging me to go to college, he only made me feel that I was 'less than.' I have become successful but always feel inferior to others."

Many of you will easily be able to identify what you were passionate about in life, and many of you will not. Some of you have held on to your passions and some of you have let them go. Some will easily remember what those passions were and some will not. To facilitate this reconnection, you may begin by asking yourself what you loved when you were a child. When you were an adolescent. Then ask yourself if what you loved is missing from your life.

Reconnecting with Your True Self

Use your journal to write the answers to the following questions. Now, remember back as far as you can . . .

What did you really love to do?

What were you really good at?

What did you want to do more than anything else in life?

What were your fantasies, dreams, visions?

What talent or "gift" do you have hidden away?

What would you do if you could start your life all over again?

What are the things you want to do before you die?

What makes you happy?

What are your unrealized goals?

What would you say was your greatest regret?

What has been your purpose/goal in life?

Have you fulfilled yourself as an individual?

Whose voice stopped you? Yours? Your parents'? Both? In what ways?

If you could speak to either your mother or father about this now, what would you say?

Was there something about your personality that failed to thrive?

Does whatever makes you special, or uniquely "you," still exist?

In what ways are you like your mother and father?

In what ways are you dissimilar from your mother and father?

Did your mother and father have "passions"? What were they?

What lessons did you learn about "passions" from your parents?

Were passions to be kept in the background? Foreground?

Would you say your parents encouraged your passions or not?

What messages did you learn from your parents about the importance of being happy and satisfied in life?

Wholeness Restored

Wholeness can be restored through reclaiming energies or lost parts of the self. The status of the self will change and grow. Matt, age 56, commented, "When I began developing my physical attributes again I began to feel young. Despite the pain I was in, my mind told me I was like a teenager, throwing that ball around. It didn't matter that I had to slow down, it only mattered that I felt the thrill of the ball in my hand and heard the whoosh of it hitting the bottom of the net."

The power within loss is the ability to reestablish the parts that have been hidden. This becomes a positive force for rebuilding your self-concept. Throughout history, orphans have demonstrated an extraordinary ability to use themselves creatively. This ability can be attributed to a kind of "will to power," that rises from loss and results in creative function.[3]

Are you surprised that you have lived so long without the missing parts of yourself now? Did you find something new about yourself? The most common categories described by people when they were asked what part of them had been recovered were the following:

➤ The creative part of self

➤ The artistic part of self

> ➤ A more mature part of self

> ➤ The responsible part of self

> ➤ A compassionate part of self that is interested in other people

> ➤ A part of self that appreciated nature

> ➤ A part of self interested in business

> ➤ The recovery of some talent

> ➤ The ability to think freely

> ➤ An emotional part of self

Changes were experienced in a variety of ways, including those listed below:

Physical. Physical acuity, the love of movement, sports—skiing, bike riding, running, skipping, tennis, golf, archery, Ping-Pong, flying airplanes, canoeing—dance, exercise, jazzercise, karate, Pilates, yoga, mechanical skills, carpentry.

Emotional. Deep feelings, laughing, crying, intuition.

Intellectual. Ability to think more clearly for self, the ownership of cognition and rationality, the appreciation of mental processes, the ability to have and share new ideas, reading, rereading books from the past, spending time in the library.

Compassionate. Loving more people, loving more deeply, needing people more, loving unconditionally, learning to praise others, having charitable feelings, developing the ability to sustain judgment while another feeling emerges.

Creative. All creative abilities such as singing, dancing, painting, drawing, scrap-booking, photography, playing musical instruments, learning and speaking languages, photography, writing prose and poetry, inspiring self and others.

Spiritual. Deeper awareness of spirit and soul, deepening of human relationships, studying healing arts, looking at perspective of "other" rather than self, religious practices, studying other religions, meditation, astronomy, astrology, widening world view, becoming more concerned about own death and therefore own life, embracing own mortality.

Deepening of the Self Can Make the Soul Speak

As you reconnect to your birth self and its lost parts, the unity of the self is reestablished and you begin to feel stronger, more real, more yourself, and more self-reliant. Those with a developed spiritual sense feel strongly that their souls—the part of themselves that had been alive from their beginnings and had made them uniquely who they were—were being recognized. It was orphanhood that had provided them with the opportunity to develop because they had become able to freely make life choices.

> Sam, age 54, expressed it this way: "When I returned to 'me,' I was making the only choice available to me after my parents died. It was a return to my *self,* to my soul. Those words all represent the same concept, 'me' is the psychological term, and 'soul' is the spiritual term, but they are as one. I think of 'soul' as the vessel that holds my strivings, aspirations, proclivities, and inherent nature. Everything that ultimately defined me was now available to me. I had access to myself. In some ways I had hidden parts of myself while still their child, now there was no longer the same rationale for falseness."

Many people expressed a freedom to be themselves and express their "souls" for the first time.

> Marsha, age 57, said: "I felt as though I lost my parents but I gained a soul-driven perspective on life. I was in charge completely and I felt both lost and, at the same time, directed from within. It was a strange blending of opposites. My soul is what is inside of me and has been since my birth. It carries all the information about who I am, not unlike my DNA, but it is not possible to see it or test it. My parents' presence affected everything in my life. With them absent, I am soul driven."

This notion of becoming soul-driven was comfortable for many of the people who revealed their lives for this book. Dan, age 37, said, "My inner drives, coming from my soul, were set free a long time ago, I listened to them but never acted on them. My orphanhood presented me with the time to begin acting on what I felt deeply to be my inner self/soul."

We all begin thinking about our souls in midlife because we are getting older. As we see the years going by, we feel the need to live differently, with more meaning, more deeply. Naturally, as we deepen our perspective we will start feeling and talking about our "souls," which is the deepest feature of our beingness.

> Rob, age 67, had this to say: "There is also something organic about the soul, natural and present from the beginning, which makes it essential and authentic. Learning to trust the soul and its strivings seems to be a perk of orphanhood. If there is anything absolutely divine about not having parents, it is the freedom to do what the soul wants. I mean, could my parents ever have accepted my wanting to have a salmon farm and live in Iceland? I don't think so. Would I ever have taken the risk and moved there while they were alive? I don't think so!"

I know these things from my own experience in life. I wanted to dance. My soul was that of a dancer, and it wanted expression. Frustrated for years, I have no idea what my life would have been like if I had let my dancer out freely. That is a loss. Many of you will have similar losses. Yet we all have the opportunity to make the best of what we *do* have, and we may find ourselves with a whole new range of life choices that come from orphanhood.

Who Am I Now?

Becoming whole changes your self-concept. It changes everything about how you feel about yourself—how you see yourself, how you perceive yourself, which parts of yourself seek satisfaction and expression. You will begin to answer the age-old question, Who am I? in a different way than you would have before.

Women Feel; Men Act

> Rather than leading to a vulnerable self, action-oriented coping may enhance immediate mastery and bolster self-esteem.[4]

The males I spoke with demonstrated action-oriented coping with death in the following ways:

> I encouraged my wife and children to move to a different neighborhood after my parents died.

> I started a new business.

> I worked hard to maintain control for my family.

> I bought a new car.

> I painted my own house.

> I was determined to keep everything the same.

It is likely that because men cope with grief and loss differently from women, they may not be as inclined to want to make the changes women want to make. In the domain of bereavement for men, four themes appear: controlling the expression of grief; taking action, like calling the family attorney rather than experiencing the feelings of loss; cognition, that is, finding meaning in the value of the life of the lost parent; and keeping their sadness private.[5]

Men more often strive to control their loss experience. Men want to think and act, whereas women are more willing to experience their feelings. In addition, women will more often want to share their feelings with their friends and family. Mike, age 50, commented: "When our father died, my sister Pattie and I coped very differently. She cried openly, while I did not. She shared her pain with others, while I kept mine inside. She would often become overwhelmed by emotion, while I was the one to handle financial and estate matters. She was much more comfortable than I discussing her feelings and the changes in her life."

Here is a short list of differences between male and female sibling reactions to the death of their father:

SISTER	BROTHER
"I moved."	"I did nothing."
"I quit being a lawyer."	"I kept the same career."
"I separated from my husband."	"I got married."
"I resumed my interest in art."	"I went on a vacation."
"I took over the family business."	"I handled the family business legal matters."
"I took Mom in."	"I visited Mom and my sister more."

Examine Sibling Reactions

Use your journal to write the answers to the following questions.

Look at your own family. What effects did the deaths of your parents have on your brother(s)? sister(s)?

What have you witnessed about the differences in reactions between a close friend of yours and their sibling(s) to parental death?

Have you discussed the death of your own parents with your sibling(s)?

Being Invisible

What many respondents to my questions revealed was the following sequence. First, they began to recognize how their "selves" were changing as a result of the loss of their parents. Then they began to adjust to the subsequent change in power, authority, and the attendant freedom. Finally, they were able to revisit the issue of how "invisible" their true selves had been and to come to terms with this invisibility. This was a realization that brought them feelings of remorse and pain. Commented Amy, age 43: "I had forgotten how much my own mother and father did not 'get' who I was. It is such a shame, because I am pretty great now, and I don't know how I kept myself from being me (and great) long ago. . . . It was a combination effect; they wanted me to be good and I wanted to please. I was immature and certainly not self-assertive enough."

In Chapter 2 of this book, I discussed the issues of the self and its authentic versus its false nature. Suffice it to say for now that orphanhood presents an opportunity for the self to become reestablished and restored. Self-recognition is the first step. The next steps include choosing what parts to express and learning how to express them. Making lists is helpful. Respondents reported feelings of guilt, sadness, remorse, anger, and depression in regard to feeling invisible to their parents. "They never knew the real me" was a common response. Or "If they had known me we would have been closer and I would have felt much more authentic." Or "Maybe the reason I have felt a low-level depression all my life was because of this—never feeling seen by Mom and Dad."

In addition, these same people felt the loss as a personal one. "It's too bad I was never more myself." Or "I feel so strong, I wish I could have been this person earlier." Or "It certainly is bittersweet, this experience of having so much of me after losing so much of them." The loss of possibility is replaced with a gain of possibility. If you feel you were less than yourself in the past, you certainly are able to gain yourself in the present.

Often people feel that their new strengths would have been appreciated by their parents. "This new sense of 'taking charge' could have helped enormously in dealing with Mom's physicians." Making important decisions regarding parents' care is easier when you feel strong and determined, rather than little and unsure. All the subsequent demands on your time and energy will be more skillfully handled when you are feeling more powerful rather than less. The mere action of losing your parents has affected you in this strangely positive way.

The Wish List

It can be helpful to use your journal to make a list of the things about yourself you would like to reclaim—a kind of wish list. These are things other people have included in their wish lists:

> ➤ I wish I could be more self-sufficient.

> ➤ I wish I could be happier.

> ➤ I wish I could be more satisfied with myself.

> ➤ I wish I could be less practical.

> ➤ I wish I could be a sculptress.

> ➤ I wish I had more time to play golf.

> ➤ I wish I could retire and write books.

> ➤ I wish I were healthier.

> ➤ I wish I were able to laugh things off.

> ➤ I wish I were lighthearted.

> ➤ I wish for more time to spend on vacations with my family.

> ➤ I wish I had a better marriage.

> ➤ I wish I had a closer relationship with my extended family.

> ➤ I wish I could stop thinking so much.

> ➤ I wish I could go back to school.

> ➤ I wish I could move to Paris.

> ➤ I wish I could move back home.

> ➤ I wish I could live with my daughter again.

> ➤ I wish I could sing.

> ➤ I wish I could become a photographer.

➤ I wish I could be the person I want to be.

➤ I wish I were more loving.

➤ I want to write a song.

➤ I want to climb the highest peak and meditate there.

➤ I wish I could live in the country.

Make a wish list of your own and feel free to include things you find in this list. After you have completed your wish list, write out a plan of action that will satisfy the goals you have set for yourself.

Converting Desire into Action

Bringing ideas and notions into action is an important aspect of this change process. Anything you can do to help yourself along is good. Remember: What prevents you from changing after your parents have died are feelings of guilt or fear. How you can benefit from this loss is a subject that often produces negative feelings. Give yourself permission to grow, or find someone who will give you permission if you cannot give it to yourself.

Giving Up Your Childhood

After spending years with patients and interviewees discussing the impact of parent loss, I have concluded that this is a time in life that is ripe for many transitions:

Losing family history

Losing family contact

Redefining your self

Shifting roles of power and authority

Reclaiming goals and becoming fully adult

Feeling more responsible

Feeling life's finiteness

Sensing your own mortality

Learning to let go of past parental conflicts

Learning to appreciate the finer things in life—love, people, nature, and the beauty of life itself

Mainly, the transition from "childhood" to life after the death of your parents is a shift in psychological readiness for life; and life for the person who has lost his or her parents presents an open page upon which to write whatever words suit your own purpose. You move into more responsibility and find an opportunity to express yourself and your dreams more fully. Once your self has been restored, you can move into a new approach to relationships that is a large departure from your self-centered approach to life in the past.

There are gains and losses in life, and this is certainly true of the transition from being someone's child to nobody's child. As you lose your innocence, you gain consciousness; as you lose insecurity, you gain authority; as you lose indecision, you gain leadership; as you lose irresponsibility and gain dominance, you lose childhood and gain self. And you lose parents and gain inner courage, insight, and strength. What a mixed blessing!

As odd as it may seem, life after the death of parents may be the most rewarding time of your life. You have graduated, so to speak. You will learn that you can take on a new role. You will recognize new capabilities. You will find the silver lining in the cloud of loss. You are free to be yourself.

7

The Sky's the Limit:
Transformation in Action

*Of the desires expressed, the one which is most right
is the desire to be "master of oneself," because
without this nothing else is possible.*

—G. I. Gurdjeff

T hus far in this book, you have been encouraged to understand how your self was affected by your environment, how your self developed and was expressed within your family; and how your self functioned within your family structure. Most important, you have been encouraged to understand how, at the time of your parents' deaths, your self can grow, become restored, and develop once again.

Five Steps to the New Self

1. Reenvision
2. Restore
3. Rekindle
4. Restructure
5. Renew

The New Self

"Adaptation is the individual giving energy to establishing a new way of life with a new potential for satisfaction and goal attainment."[1] This is the time for you to give yourself energy. In your own experience of adapting, you will find yourself inclined to behave differently, as though a new program had been inserted into your brain and was directing your actions. As someone without parents now, the self can and will change. Renewing the self becomes a process filled with potential and possibility.

Changes You've Experienced

The following are short writing exercises for your journal to focus your attention on the changes you have experienced as a result of losing your parents.

➤ Describe your past self.

➤ Describe your present self.

One of the aspects of the renewed self is in the power that this self has in regard to existing relationships. There is a corresponding commitment to new relationships.[2] The bereaved individual tends to say to him- or herself, "Well, I'm not going to let this go. After all, I've already had enough loss, and I now so much value this person with whom I am involved." What connects people becomes all the more important in light of how you now feel about yourself and others. Human feelings, emotions, needs, and values outweigh in importance patterns of psychological distancing as a way to stay safe or alone. The emotions of grief weave back and forth from shock to sorrow, from acceptance to disbelief, sometimes making it difficult to predict how you will feel in any one day. What might begin as a lovely morning may be turned around by a flash of memory of your parent, or by seeing someone who resembles your lost mother. An awareness of loss is always present. It can be mediated by a phone call to someone you care about. Reconnecting to good feelings helps you feel less isolated. It is a symbolic turning toward life. And deeper and more meaningful relationships help to assuage the empty feelings of loss.

New relationships have the advantage of enabling you to begin again. There is a longing for someone else to have meaning for you or to care about you in a special way. There can be such panic when you envision a life without that someone to treasure and to love. Anyone who has lost even a pet and yearned for a new pet to help heal the hurt and loss knows what this means. Psychologists agree there is a need to replace an old relationship with a new one when loss of the first relationship occurs. "If my mother had not died, I never would have married!" confessed a man in his fifties. He told me during our interview that never before had he felt the need for, or allowed, such a deep commitment. "I felt free to love for the first time . . ." admitted a colleague of mine in his late thirties, soon after he had lost his last parent.

Normative growth typically involves development from a "narcissistic orientation" toward a relationship with an "other." Although personal transformation during this time of life is unique and individualized, the majority of the people spoken with agreed that no matter what other changes occurred, there was a shift in how relationships were perceived, in how much they meant, and in the ways they mattered. It is not uncommon for an orphan to share, "I never needed or loved like this before."

Positive Emotional Results from Grief

Some of the positive emotional results that accompany the grief of losing your parents include allowing yourself to feel:

More vulnerable/needy

More compassionate/sensitive

More whole/fulfilled

More mature/responsible

More loving/more in need of love

All of these feelings and emotions create a more open and engaging atmosphere for relationships with people who matter to you.

Another Side of Having No Parents

It is important to acknowledge that feelings are mixed. For example, in addition to a heightened sense of the ability to love, the following are also common experiences that lead to needing and valuing relationships:

The sense of being bereft

An unexpected loneliness

A deeply personal sense of isolation

An unexpected sense of abandonment

Changed Perceptions

Below are some of the statements people have made about perceived changes in their relationships:

"I had the sense that the world was forever changed, and so was how I looked at all the people in my life. They were all vulnerable now, they could all die, and I was going to appreciate them more than ever."

"I felt as though I had lost my best friends and my aloneness was stark. I reached out to others more than in the past."

"I became intensely aware of how much I needed other people now. I looked forward to spending time with others much more."

"I used to be falsely independent; after my parents died, I relished my 'dependent' nature and allowed myself to need, to feel my needs, to express my needs."

"I am so thankful for all the support I received from my friends when my parents died. I don't think I would have managed as well as I did without them."

"I stopped taking my siblings for granted; I wanted to get to know them as adults."

"I knew my sister would never forget the troubles we had our entire life together; I gave up on her, but I started new relationships with women from my place of worship and I am getting closer to them."

"I realized I needed a male buddy; where do you find one of those in your fifties?"

"Skin and bones, that's how I felt, just raw, raw, raw! I wanted lots of hugs from people."

Changes in Values Happen First

The shift in what is perceived as important comes from the experience of loss itself, the feeling of aloneness, the awareness of mortality, the appreciation of life. The process can take place like this:

> ➤ First, you lose your parent. There is an immediate shift toward feeling more vulnerable. You experience this as feeling abandoned, lonely, insecure, fearful, being scared of the future, being indecisive, not knowing what to do, and missing your parent.

> ➤ Next, you mourn your loss and begin the process of grieving. Along the way you begin to notice you are reacting differently to things, responding differently to people. You are feeling more sensitive. "I knew I was in trouble when I saw a large truck hit a squirrel in the road and I started to cry."

➤ Your values are changing; you are less in a hurry. You want to slow down and find value in living every day. You don't really know how long *you* have to live now. You want to make each second count.

➤ You feel an urgency to live life to the fullest. You have witnessed death, you want life. "I can no longer wait for my marriage to improve, it is not going to! I want a change now!"

➤ You make the choice of life; living.

➤ Your senses have been awakened. Nature is much more important to you. You seek natural spaces to visit. Your sensitivities and eyes have been opened. Your heart has been opened.

➤ You begin to value highly all the people you are close to and love.

Or, the following can take place:

➤ You lose your parent and you feel bad, sad, experience a degree of discomfort, but you were not really close to your parent, or you were still conflicted about the relationship, and you are left feeling guilt, anger, resentment.

➤ You grieve, but your parent was not the most important person for you as a parent is, perhaps, for someone else, someone who described the relationship with his or her parent as close.

➤ You adjust.

➤ You move forward.

➤ Personal changes may or may not occur.

You are an individual and have had unique experiences throughout your life. It is the same with loss, grief, and transformation. What is the same for everyone is the potential for change of some sort.

Things to Remember

> There is more than one type of parent relationship.
>
> There is more than one type of loss.
>
> There is more than one type of grief.
>
> There is more than one type of change.

Many people are extremely surprised when they realize the extent of their grief over the loss of their parents. Parents are expected to die before you do; nevertheless, the extent of the grief can be shocking and different from what you would have assumed. Loss is one of the most difficult human experiences—if not the most difficult—to endure. It should be no surprise when the loss of your parents throws you into a major tailspin.

What seem to be soothing are expressions of loving, caring, nurturing, and support from others. At no other time is an expression of caring from another person as healing as it is now. The support you receive from your other family members, spouse, and friends can help you through what is a major life transition.

> Maddie, age 46, commented: "I couldn't have made it without my friends and husband. . . . The days I was immobilized they helped me take care of my responsibilities."

Needing the "Other"

When you have lost one or both of your primary bond relationships, Mom and/or Dad, the physical bond has been severed even though the spiritual bond remains. Losing the physical bond is quite painful and noteworthy. It was your parents who provided unconditional love and support. Although they still exist on a spiritual and symbolic level, they are physically absent. The support and sense of belonging you enjoyed when they were alive have been removed.

In place of these relationships you receive the potential reward of independence, personal strength, and growth. Yet, the loss of these very important primary relationships leaves you in need of other relationships. This newly identified appreciation for others translates into deeply welcoming other human beings into your life and heart.

"I need people now in a different way," reported Sammy, age 36, after her last parent died. Here are other types of responses:

"I feel like I need people, for the first time."

"My need for others feels deeper."

"I am aware of wanting and needing to reach out to others, like I didn't do before."

"My sense of need has changed; it's bigger."

"Something has changed; I am more tolerant of others and more patient with my wife and children, and their moods and needs."

"I feel the need for personal contact with my friends more than before."

Needing Relationship

It is curious, but often with the loss of parents the bereaved begin to experience life in terms of "relationship to" more than in the past. Examples include: relationship to yourself, relationship to others, relationship to the memory of your parents, relationship to your extended family, relationship to your own children, relationship to others whom you may love, and relationship to life itself. There is an existential shift in life philosophy. This shift occurs because as you begin to deal with the issues related to parent death that have been discussed in this book (such as changes in role, awareness of mortality, more responsibility, feelings of remorse over lost reparation with parents, and so on), there is a life awareness that "something is very different now."

Changing from being someone's child with the emphasis on yourself—perhaps even in a self-centered or selfish way—occurs when you are without parents and you find yourself emphasizing your need for others. It becomes important to spend time with other people, to bond to others, and to be considerate of them. The pain of being alone is severe enough to cause you to reestablish priorities, and among these is the need for people.

> Marta, age 38, commented: "Never before in my life did my friends and family members become as important to me as when Mom and Dad both died. I needed to feel a part of a unit; these people became terribly important to me."

The meaning of everything can change after your parents have died. Life feels more tenuous; you feel more vulnerable; life is more precious; close relationships become more important. The meaning of life is clearer. Death becomes real. Your own death becomes a distinct possibility; you are the next in line. What you value now becomes real, whether what you value is people, animals, relationships, spirit, your beliefs, or God.

> Barbara, age 54, put it this way: "As miserable as I was after Mom died, I can remember looking outside at the trees and they seemed greener than I had remembered. Even in my grief, I felt vulnerable, open, and in touch with everyone."

The loss of the parental "relationship" is a separate factor from the loss of the person. Just as there is grief over the loss and a feeling of deprivation because the lost person no longer exists to nourish or love you, there is the loss of the relationship that had kept you sound and functioning in a human sense. Understanding our need for attachment and closeness makes us understand the depth of loss more clearly. The loss of the parental relationship, which is not comparable to any other relationship, leaves a gap that is in actuality impossible to fill. In a way, the only solace is to fill the gap with the self and some aspect of it that couldn't have entered before.

The Strength of Vulnerability

At your most vulnerable, you experience the most need, feeling, emotion, intensity of experience. Certainly, losing your parents is such a time. There are many times in life when we feel the "most vulnerable."

Any crisis can produce this kind of deepening of feeling. It is the deepening of feeling that makes you begin to think about your eventual old age, your mortality, your days left and what to do with them to make the most out of every day.

"Everything changed when my mother died: Everything, it all changed." This was a comment from a 45-year-old man who owned his own business and was quite successful. He described his mother as someone who gave herself to her family and never held anything back. "My whole life changed, from my children seeing their grandmother, to my father having no one to live with, from every minute being different than it used to be. At first I cried and broke down a lot. Now, I am just left with this incredible loss. Do I feel free? No! There was nothing to be free from. My mom was so cool, I did everything I wanted."

The experience of adult loss creates an unhappy atmosphere that makes people feel extremely vulnerable. Most agree that even though they do not enjoy the experience of vulnerability, it is an experience not without its positive attributes, such as a renewed sense of life purpose and direction, strength and power, feelings of softness and love for others. It is part of this transitional time in life, and it motivates you toward action.

Even though vulnerability makes people uncomfortable, sustaining the feelings of vulnerability creates the opportunity for you to become a stronger person. Sustaining feelings of vulnerability:

➤ Promotes a sense of power

➤ Allows introspection

➤ Sparks ideas

➤ Creates an atmosphere for sharing with others

Barbara, age 56, said, "It was ultimately my vulnerability that led me through my changes. I wanted to change jobs, but I was afraid. I felt a lot of anxiety. Instead of giving in and doing nothing, I continued to allow myself to feel scared and explored new job possibilities. It was a difficult time for me and I had to do a lot of personal exploration, but my feeling of wanting more in life kept me going. My vulnerability put me in touch with myself."

Mike, age 48, said, "After my mother died, my feeling of sensitivity increased, and it was unusual for me to feel that way. At first I didn't like how I felt. I didn't think it was manly to feel that way. Sometimes I even felt embarrassed. Still, I stuck with it and realized that I had the ability to direct my own life and the power to make things happen."

Barbara and Mike are both talking about how productive it is when feelings of vulnerability are not pushed away. When vulnerability is allowed to surface, dealt with consciously, and sustained, feelings of self-reliance and accomplishment are the result.

Marriage and Other Long-Term Intimate Relationships

All relationships seem to be affected by the death of a loved one, and the death of parents can cause great upheaval and turmoil. Marriages are generally affected in one of two ways; they either improve or begin a process of disintegration. Yes, there are some that remain stable as they have always been. "As with changes within other relationships, those that affect spouses can be favorable, unfavorable, or ambiguous."[3] When there is improvement in a marriage, it is typically because of a supportive attitude from the partner who has not been bereaved. The partner who suffered the loss feels the partner was "there for me when I needed him\her," was "to be counted on," "took up the slack," or was generally considerate, kind, helpful, and supportive.

When marriages improve it is because of the support, caring, and love given to the bereaved. This care can be expressed in a number of ways, from quietly listening to actively holding the other; from helping with funeral arrangements to packing up personal items; from driving the bereaved to appointments to making dinner for the family. As a result, the bond between the married partners grows and becomes stronger. The bereaved has a need for help, and the supportive partner fills that need. Here are some ways partners responded:

My husband comforted me when I cried.

My wife told me she understood my pain and loss.

My husband relieved me of daily errands and cooking.

My wife came to the office and brought me lunch.

My husband took me on a vacation.

Pat, age 36, had this to say: "After my mom died, Mike made dinner every night of the week, and, with the help of our kids, did the dishes. I will always love him for that. In addition, he was kind, considerate of my feelings and stress, and placed no demands on me. We cuddled a lot and his hugs soothed my deep feelings of pain."

When marriages were improved, certainly the issues of vulnerability and need played a role in the change. "A large number of people reported their marriages and partnerships had grown substantially stronger in the aftermath of parental death. These respondents seemed to make a greater emotional investment in their romantic attachments, investments that were, for the most part, largely rewarded."[4]

In this study by Debra Umberson, various issues regarding the strength of relationships during grief and the effects of grief on marital relationships were tested with interesting results. Umberson's study concluded that

> compared with the relationships of individuals who have not recently lost a parent, the relationships of individuals who recently experienced a mother's death are characterized by a decline in social support from their partners and by an increase in the partners' negative behaviors. The relationships of individuals who recently experienced a father's death are characterized by a decline in relationship harmony and an increase in relationship strain and frequency of conflict.

While there were respondents who provided appreciative and warm reports of a supportive spouse who made the bereavement process easier, many respondents provided detailed accounts that give insight into the processes behind the quantitative reports of a decline in marital quality following bereavement.

The five themes of marital strain and decline that were identified with the greatest frequency were:

1. Failed social support

2. Partner's unwillingness or inability to communicate about the death

3. Partner's lack of empathy

4. Excessive expectations and demands by the partner

5. Liberation[5]

This can occur because of the nature of the choice of spouse (that is, was it a good choice for the individual, or was the choice of spouse made to please a doting parent). "In some cases, marriages and partnerships weakened or were scuttled. Parental death catapulted these offspring into scrutinizing their relationships and seriously considering whether or not they wanted to spend the rest of their lives with their partners—life being, they now realized, astonishingly short."[6]

Grief heightens emotions and when emotions are running high, all of your relationships will be affected. Particularly with your intimate "others" there is the chance of becoming too demanding, excessively needy, irritable, or critical. The demands of bereavement are grave and sometimes make individuals feel like they cannot cope with their lives or their spouses' needs. People commonly ask this question without being able to find an acceptable answer: "How can I take proper care of my own family when I am in such pain and despair?" Spouses often feel that the ailing and now deceased parent has "taken time away from me," which certainly stresses the marital relationship.

Carol, age 39, says: "John was always jealous of my connection to my family, always felt left out and insignificant to them. I am surprised my marriage lasted through the many years of both of my parents' illnesses. The time it took for me to manage their affairs after they died really stressed my life at home. John was not supportive; rather felt left out and angry all of the time. I may never be able to forget about how he acted, even the day of the funeral. We were so disconnected, and I really needed his support . . . but didn't get it."

On the other hand the death of a parent can put an end to an emotionally and physically compelling time that drains energy. When caregiving ends, being relieved of the added responsibility typically helps to ease the strain in the marriage. Stories like Carol's are common, unfortunately, and contribute to the creation of future problems for the marriage. Is the marital stress due to internal and preexisting marital conflict? Is the marital stress due to consequences of bereavement? Some of the negative effects of parental death on marriage contribute to psychological distress, alcohol consumption, and the decline of physical health.

Failed Social Support

When the partner of the bereaved fails to meet emotional needs, it can lead to feelings of anger, frustration, and disappointment with the partner. Sometimes the partner, who is typically comforting or supportive, fails to provide such nourishment in this specific situation, perhaps because of the intensity of the circumstance or the specificity of the subject matter—death, parental death to be specific.

Cathy, age 41, comments: "On top of me being so miserable about losing Mom, my husband wasn't emotionally available. He disappeared, which made everything so much worse for me."

Johnny, age 57, says: "There must have been something losing my father brought up for my wife. She was usually there for me, but for some reason she would not discuss my grief over my father."

Unwillingness to Communicate

The ability to discuss the loss is important for the bereaved. When one of the partners in the marriage fails to talk with the other, not only does the relationship suffer, but the loss and feeling of emptiness intensifies. Cathy is an example: "Every time I wanted to talk to my husband he turned a deaf ear. So on top of grief I had to deal with frustration and anger."

Due to the sensitive nature of your newly experienced orphan vulnerability your need for closeness intensifies. When you are unable to talk to your spouse about your feelings, it becomes a very uncomfortable situation. The spouse who is unwilling to communicate during these times may have a problem dealing with intense emotions or may have an issue with the whole idea of death and grief. It can leave the bereaved feeling even more alone. This may highlight an existing marital conflict.

Empathy

Empathy, compassion, and emotional support are the gifts of a loving relationship. When this exists for a couple in crisis, there is nothing more valuable. Sue, age 52, said, "My husband was wonderful throughout my mother's illness, death, and all the subsequent changes in our life. He was a saint."

Sue's husband was a model for empathy when he demonstrated these qualities:

- ➤ Openness to Sue's feelings

- ➤ Ability to be there for her no matter what

- ➤ Interest and support for all new activities Sue explored

- ➤ Maintaining a calm and nurturing attitude

- ➤ Modeled compassion for their children

These are other comments made by people who felt their spouses had been empathic.

"He was supportive of my changes and even if he felt threatened he let me do what I wanted."

"She liked my new friends."

"He helped me paint every room in our house."

"For the first time in years she didn't get mad at me for watching Monday Night Football."

Improved marriages were reported by people who developed new interests together, like playing golf or tennis or taking dance lessons. When both marriage partners participated in an activity, it indicated signs of an increased sense of togetherness. Many spouses supported their partners' desires to change significant things about their lives or themselves, like starting school again or changing physical characteristics with plastic surgery.

Liberation from Negative Relationships, Including Marriage

Several respondents from the Umberson study reported that marital strain eventually led to the break up of their marriages. Data suggest the marriages that end after parental death may have always been troubled, conflicted, or otherwise unsuitable in some way. Nonetheless, one fact is clear. For many people, the fact they no longer had to worry about how the parent would respond to the break up of their marriage allowed them the freedom to initiate a separation or divorce that may not have taken place before the parent's death.

To illustrate, these are some of the variables that people have reported as influencing their decisions to separate or divorce:

➤ Freedom to separate or divorce due to parental absence

➤ Expressing pressure to stay together if parent were alive still

➤ Marriage, more than a committed relationship, was always in response to parental pressure to marry someone like spouse

➤ Freedom to marry "outside" of parental expectation like religious, cultural, socioeconomic

➤ Freedom to end a marriage that provided structure or security important to parent

➤ Freedom to choose a lifestyle that may not include marriage as important

➤ Feeling of liberation experienced impulsively

➤ Feeling free to test new self in the world

➤ Ability to break from destructive or conflicted relationship patterns

Susanne, age 46, noted: "I married my husband because he was suitable, my parents liked him and he was capable of supporting me. . . . Was he a good choice for the 'inner' me? No. So, when my parents died, I left him."

Mike, age 50, said: "Everyone in my family married for social status, it was important for them. When my parents were both gone, I was free to make different choices, choices they would have disliked but which were good for me."

Lara, age 41, had this to say: "It was very clear that I married young to get out of my parents' house. I was terribly misunderstood and unhappy. Now they are gone. My choice of mate was not so good; I have decided to leave him."

Bereaved individuals react more strongly immediately following a parent's death. Strong reactions that create turmoil may eventually relax. The death of parents precipitates the urge to change life, which may eventually dissipate if the impulse is not acted upon. Waiting for time to take its course is always a good idea if you do not want to behave impulsively or precipitously. Even so, the general quality of an unsatisfactory marriage or relationship will not necessarily improve with time.

"The bereaved individual attempts to establish and extend relationships to fill the void left by the deceased person"[7] and often this is accomplished by the bereaved turning to the marriage or relationship partner for additional support. If this is not provided, there is a decline in the reported satisfaction of that relationship, resulting in marital strain or frustration. The consequences of this situation remain up to the individual to sort out and may be dependent on the ability to cope with stress or conflict generally. On the other hand, becoming "orphaned," having to manage this new stage of life with new life demands and the feeling of being liberated for the first time in life, suggests old coping mechanisms may fail and new strategies are in need of development.

Willingness to Communicate

"What I appreciated about my wife was that she kept bringing up my father's death; she didn't force me to discuss my feelings, but often she would ask me how I was feeling about my dad or how was my grief going. That way, I knew she cared and her gentle prodding disarmed my defenses," commented Tony, age 49.

The typical way for a male to grieve is alone. While women share their grief with friends and their spouses, often requiring their spouses to listen to their feelings and pain, men tend to keep their feelings private. Men often described needing to be reminded to share their feelings, or encouraged to let themselves "feel" their pain and loss. Here is a list of subtle reminders that show your spouse you are interested:

➤ How are you doing with your loss?

➤ Have you given any thought to your mother/father lately?

➤ I have been thinking about your mother/father myself lately . . .

➤ What have your thoughts been?

➤ Today was a day of memory about your mother/father for me, how about you?

➤ You haven't mentioned your loss lately; I am interested in listening if you would like to talk.

> ➤ I know you have been thinking about your mother/father, do you want to share any of it?

> ➤ You have been busy with issues related to your parent's death. Can I help in any way?

New Marriages

In the face of aloneness and in the wake of orphanhood, some people will marry. Marriage can be motivated by the need to connect to someone, to feel a part of another person, to end the deep sense of isolation orphanhood can bring.

A marriage that occurs at this stage of life can be rewarding and fulfilling. If the loss of parents coincides with a shift in the psychological environment of the bereaved so that parental issues are no longer suffocating the ability to wisely select a partner, the results will be very good. When I asked a confirmed bachelor what changes his parents' deaths might portend, he said, "I will probably finally marry someone."

Some people feel freer to marry after their parents die because the kind of person they want to marry would not have been acceptable to their parents. This may have been due to differences in race, ethnicity, social class, or religious background. What their parents may have thought "suitable" for them in their choice of a mate did not match their own need or desire. Feeling older can often result in someone wanting to get married so they can share their life with someone else.

> Said Sam, age 47: "I had been dating this woman for two years and despite all the time I resisted marriage, after my mother who was my last parent died, I felt strongly that my time had come. It was time to create a bond to someone. I am certain it had to do with my loss."

Feeling Good Again

Grief is a process. I cannot stress this enough: It must be allowed to run its own course. No one can tell you when you are finished with grief or any of the feelings associated with grief. The notion that grief should be over quickly because "You shouldn't have been so dependent on your parent anyway" or "They were bound to die, they were old" or "How long did you think your parent would live" is unfair, unrealistic, and unnatural.

Parental relationships have been and will be always be the source of either great comfort or conflict, or something in the middle. No matter what, their power over your life cannot be disputed. To accept this situation is wise and to move on with your own life after their deaths is important for all the reasons illuminated already in this book. Recovery comes in steps and will weave itself throughout your bereavement—probably long after your parents have died.

There is no ultimate act of recovery. Recovery is a process that begins at some point in your grief process. The following list derived from statements made by dozens of people summarizes aspects of recovery:

"I began to feel better when my interest in my own hobbies returned."

"I knew hope was near because my energy returned."

"I started wanting to cook again."

"My interest in sex returned."

"I began thinking about taking a vacation with my family."

"I stopped dreading the holidays."

"I was no longer angry with my sisters."

"Even though it was soon after my dad died, I began thinking about what was possible for me to do that would make *me* feel good again."

"I woke up earlier in the morning like I used to."

"I decided to lose weight."

"I wanted to socialize again."

"I stopped feeling so angry for being left."

"I began wearing my hair like my mother."

"I stopped crying as soon as I would get in the car to drive to the cemetery, and I would only cry when I arrived."

"When I could look at pictures of my dad and not cry."

"When I stopped thinking Mom was going to walk back through the door."

"When I could talk about my parents and not become overcome with emotion or cry."

Friendships

Friends are vitally important now. They provide companionship, support, and care. Many friends will automatically "be there" for you. Yet if they are not, you can gently ask for what you need. For example, you might say, "could you come over and just hang out with me for a while?" Or you might ask, "What are you doing tomorrow night? I'd like some company." Or, "Can I come over and be with you for a while?"

Your friends may be used to you being strong and won't immediately recognize that your need for them has changed. You need to be able to tell them you have suffered a tremendous loss and you want them to be patient with you. You can tell your friends you need their help, their support, that you need them to listen and that you need help with your kids.

The need for and the appreciation of relationships suggests friendships are as affected by the deaths of parents as are marriages. Bereaved people need their friends, need support, and need to stay open to new relationships that will come. "A friend of mine wrapped her arms around a neighbor who had recently lost his mother and simply rocked him."[8]

Friends can:

➤ Visit

➤ Listen

➤ Give emotional support

➤ Provide company/make plans for activities

➤ Hang out

➤ Cook meals together

➤ Bring over meals

➤ Drive the bereaved to appointments

➤ Help with babysitting

➤ Give hugs

Joanne, age 54, commented: "If it weren't for my friends, I would have been all alone in my suffering. I had no siblings, and my friends were my support."

Alan, age 45, said: "You know who your friends are in times of stress and crisis; my male friends really were there. They didn't always talk, but I felt their presence and support."

It is more than likely that you have some friends who have already lost their parents. These friends will be able to understand your confusion and your loss with little explanation. While you may discover that a few of your friends are fair-weather friends, you will find solace and understanding from your true and lasting friendships.

Sibling Relationships

Often siblings fight and are angry with one another after their parents die. What is at the bottom of this might be anything from one sibling feeling that the other sibling got more attention to feeling that the other sibling got more material goods while the parent was still alive.

It is in these relationships that the drama of who got more love is played out. With an alarming lack of consciousness of the reasons for the battle, siblings often fight over possessions after the death of parents. It is not unusual for the battles to be uncomfortable and displeasing, even ugly. It can be particularly difficult when the battle is over some favorite possession of the family, like a certain photo, religious item, or antique. There is often no easy way to resolve this type of battle, unless the decision to share the item is made.

Time will heal some of these conflicts. Over time as siblings realize that each has suffered an equal loss, they will begin to feel some sympathy for one other. Sharing memories and events from their past will help them unite in their grief. As they feel the bond of togetherness, they will cease to feel the pain of jealousy. Just the simple fact of having suffered a common loss and having dealt with it together can draw siblings closer to one another.

When you need to be the one to heal the conflict because time on its own has not been successful, you have to be able to call on your highest self to get it done. You can rise above the conflict by:

➤ Being spiritual/compassionate/thinking about someone other than yourself

➤ Wanting to pass family items on to the next generation

You have to remember it is important to share, and it is equally important to ask for something that you want. It is perfectly okay for everyone to have something and to know that you cannot have it all. Always focus on the fact that it is the loss of your parents that has created the pain not the loss of their things. You cannot hold on to them no matter what object of theirs you now possess. Your memories of your parents will ultimately become their legacy.

It is important to remember that each sibling has suffered a loss and each is struggling with the loss in his or her unique way. Sometimes, after the battles are over, siblings realize they are the only ones left and reconnect in better ways. Siblings can also be transformed in their relationship to one another as they continue life without their parents. It is often the case that siblings will become closer after the death of their parents.

Francine, age 63, had this to say: "I didn't think I would ever talk to my sister again, after how greedy I think she became.

She hoarded all of Mom's stuff and told me she was making all the decisions without my input! . . . She always tried to take all the power, my entire life. I can remember how she would bully me as a little girl; she was older and she never let me forget it."

Whenever there are issues of power and authority between siblings, the situation is ripe for conflict. Issues may include which of them will wind up with the most property or money; which one will make decisions; which of them will go to the bank and retrieve the safety deposit box; who got there first; where is the paperwork; who had been made executor of the estate; whose feelings will be hurt by a betrayal of trust?

The process of caregiving before the death of the parent may have been difficult as well. One or two siblings may have felt they were carrying the load. Physical proximity to the parent who is sick determines which offspring will be doing the caregiving. When children do not live in the same state or country, they cannot be as involved as children that do. How each family organizes and divides the responsibilities for taking care of their parents has to be handled on an individual basis.

Sue, age 45, commented: "All of my siblings shared equally in the responsibilities of taking care of Mom and Dad."

Patty, age 36, said: "I was always the one to do everything . . ."

When interviewed and asked whether sibling relationships improved or not after parents died, the number of respondents who said yes was about the same as the number of those who said no. A factor that plays a part in any of these changes is time. Time changes everything. Over time, what might be conflicted sibling relationships may change. Over time, disturbances in marriages may change. Time changes perceptions and perceptions change behavior and attitudes. This is why it is important to take time in deciding what changes you really want to make for the long term.

Other Family Members Pitch In or Don't

The impulse to want to "recover" the lost parent by looking to another family member is not unusual. Brothers and sisters of your deceased parents can step into your parents' shoes. They may try to take on the role of your "surrogate" parent and will succeed or not to varying degrees. Your reactions will vary as well.

Here are some of the thoughts and reactions expressed about this subject:

> "My aunt (my mother's sister) was always the closest relative to me and to my mother. Naturally when Mom died, she tried as hard as she could to fill in for Mom. I will always love her for that."

> "Dad died and his older brother called my brother and told him not to worry about anything, we would always have him."

> "After my parents died, both of their siblings would call me and my sister every Sunday for a while. When they stopped we felt alone again."

> "I liked it that my aunt and uncle were doing everything they could for my brother and me, but I knew I had to grow up and not rely on anyone."

> "It helped a lot that family dinners resumed and while we missed Mom and Dad, at least the rest of us maintained contact with one another."

> "When Mom died, the four of us kids bonded closely. All we had now was each other."

> "No one in the family could replace Mom or Dad, but several of the aunts and uncles tried for a while; before they realized how impossible it would be to take on their roles."

Ultimately, as your own power and authority shifts and you begin to feel like an adult in a different way than before, you will probably resist the temptation to fall back on other family members as authority figures. Support is one thing, letting someone step into Mom's or Dad's shoes so you don't have to grow up is another thing. It is a regression.

Children

"I am always learning to appreciate my children more, and the days immediately following the death of my last parent, I looked at my children with a renewed sense of responsibility, love, and commitment to their lives. What precious people they are, I thought. What would I do if anything happened to them?" commented Maggie, age 55.

The gift of children is not to be taken lightly. When we think of those young souls we have assisted into this life, our hearts open and we are flooded with emotion. Death of parents leaves us next in line, and we begin to think about how our deaths will affect our own children. What will they feel? How can we best help them to prepare for our own demise in the future? Should we teach them to be themselves now? How might that goal be accomplished?

Reports from people who have lost their parents suggest there is progress toward more intimacy with children at this time. They need family, they appreciate their roles as parents to their children with greater passion, they seek meaning and connection, they want to model good behavior, and they feel the need to give and receive love more than ever.

Modeling "becoming yourself" is the greatest gift you can give your children. It is good for their developing and continuing self-esteem. It is terrific for your children to see you becoming or being fulfilled, self satisfied, and happy. It is fabulous for them to see you with passion for life. You are providing them with one of the following messages, and you have to decide which one it will be. "Do what you want." Or "Do what I want you to do." Hopefully, it is the first.

New Relationships

There are many factors that contribute to the initiation of new relationships, including:

> ➤ The drive to recover from grief

> ➤ The need to establish a new identity

> ➤ The need to dive into self and attach to someone interesting, perhaps someone with similarities

> ➤ The need to replace the lost love object

> ➤ The need to find someone who is felt to be a pal or a soulmate

> ➤ The need to express the need for relationship with another

> ➤ The need to begin again

> ➤ The expression of "wholeness" with another

> ➤ The need to find someone new without a reference to your past

The most dramatic story I heard came from a woman. (Of course, women share more about their romantic experiences.)

Cathy lost her father 20 years before losing her mother. Cathy lived in a large city with her husband and three children. Two of her children were in college and one was slightly disabled and in a school for children with special needs. Cathy was a career woman and was successful at what she did. I say that to assure you she was strong, efficient, a hard worker, and tended to put her career before her family from time to time. She would have described herself as caring, conscientious, loyal, trustworthy, and a humanitarian.

She admitted that an affair she had with a coworker immediately after the death of her mother was shocking because of her previous moral rectitude and provincial behavior. It was something she was embarrassed about despite the fact that the relationship was life-altering.

She had known the man for several years and had been his friend throughout his difficult and expensive divorce. She identified her vulnerability after her mother died and admitted to having had feelings for him long before the affair began. She was attracted to him for many qualities that were missing in her own husband. The friendship between the two was a source of communication and comfort. After her mother's death, Cathy began working later hours to avoid the rigors of home life, which had become painful because of her loss. Her mother had lived nearby and had come for dinner several times a week and babysat for their youngest child, and her weekly absence served as a constant reminder of what was now gone forever.

"Until now I have had an ordinary life," she said.

Cathy lost herself in work. As she began to spend more time with this other man she described the process of being in the relationship with him as different from any other prior relationship. She was vulnerable because of the loss of her mother. She attached herself to this man and described their connection as soulful and deep. They both felt like they had known each other before, a sign of familiarity and security. Her reports of their intimacy together sounded passionate and loving. The affair did not last long, no longer than 6 months. As a result of it, Cathy reported being a changed person.

She was more open; she wanted more out of life and love. She was afraid to get divorced. She was uncertain about the impact of divorce on her children. Yet, she felt as though she yearned for the kind of love and connection she had felt. She described feeling more human need than before, more need for all the soft feelings in life. She felt as though she had been exposed in some primitive way with this person and liked the raw quality she experienced. She became a better mother and a better friend.

When the affair was over, the two remained friends but within 2 years he left the company and they lost contact with each other. "I am permanently changed now," she said. "I will never be the old me. I grew in that relationship, and I have benefited from all the rewards I reaped. All that I accomplished was worth the guilt and remorse. I guess I gave myself permission to explore life after Mom died. I felt ripped off and I wanted something put back."

"I now feel I am extraordinary because of the process of receiving love that I experienced. Did it really take my mother's dying for me to know love and all the dimensions of feeling and emotion I learned as a result?"

Self-Definition

What was life altering for Cathy was her recognition of personal need, her feeling of rawness and emotion, her ability to be intimate with a man, and her openhearted reaction at the termination of the relationship. However, the most significant transformation was the loving relationship she was now capable of experiencing and sharing with another. Furthermore, her new attitude generalized into an appreciation for all of her relationships.

She also realized and admitted that her closeness to her parents had in some way stalled her personal development in the area of needing others. She had spent so much energy on her parents and family, she didn't have time for others or for herself. There was some relief on her part to be freed from family bondage.

Additionally, she felt that her choice of a lover was made from her heart/body/soul and not her mind. Her head and mind had steered her choices in the past. "He would be an appropriate or suitable partner for me," she would say. Or, "My parents would love or approve of him." Despite her success in the business world, her personal world still suffered from all sorts of past inhibitions and restrictions. So many people choose the "wrong" mate for so many reasons, not the least of which is seeking parental approval.

The other aspect of Cathy's transformation was that she felt more self-defined after both of her parents had passed away, and in some fundamental way this affected how she behaved in this new relationship. She felt "whole" and it was her "wholeness" that became attracted to him and attracted him to her at the same time. When wholeness exists where once there was suppression and repression of self there is an increase in the options from which to choose, and the relationships developed on this principle feel qualitatively different from any prior experience.

"I felt as though I was more present than ever before, that finally someone knew the real me and I felt as though I was home." I will never forget those days I spent with him and feel permanently changed as a result. Whether my friends or family notice that I am different, I do not know. I feel myself to be and that is all that matters."

Sex, Sexuality, and Passion

Of all the behaviors suppressed by human beings, sex, sexuality, and passion are on the top of the list. Sex is the physical act, sexuality is your feeling and attitude about sex, and passion is the force with which you express it all. These three elements can come to life when you are freed from your own inhibitions; a liberating effect of parental death. You may also notice a change in your sex drive, sexual satisfaction, and sensuality. If your own experience of parental oppression affected how you functioned sexually in any regard, you are now ready for a pleasant surprise.

Many of the people with whom I spoke described a much more active sex life after their parents had passed away. The reasons are fairly obvious, as is the overall assumption that when you graduate from childhood to full adulthood, one of the signposts of maturity is sexuality. Sex is for adults, and the psyche opens to the possibility quite naturally. Internal inhibitions that are a carryover from parental or family dogma need to be explored either with a help of a therapist or some other capable professional.

Here are a few of the comments made about sex by people I worked with or interviewed:

"I felt guilty enjoying sex right after my dad died; I also wondered if he was watching me."

"Sexuality between my husband and myself was always good. But I did feel freer to explore my sexual feelings after both of my parents were gone. Not immediately after, but several years later. I didn't really think about it either, just one day I noticed I felt different."

"Sex was always a way for me to relax. My wife asked me if I felt too upset to have sex and I said no. I can remember the first time after the funeral and I think I enjoyed it more than usual, but I never thought about why."

"I know for a fact sex started being better. First of all, I became sexually free."

"I made a list of all the things I wanted to do after being orphaned. Becoming more of a sexual person was on the list. I wasn't sure about how to accomplish the goal, but I was willing to work on it."

"For me, my whole sexual nature opened up."

More specifically, our love and sexual nature are typically driven by deep connection to another. When as adults, orphans, liberated people, you become motivated to share yourself deeply with another person, in true appreciation of the wonder of relationship, the opening of sexuality into your life can nourish you and your partner.

For so many in our culture, sensuality, passion, deep connection, and the behaviors that represent them have suffered damage. This damage has usually occurred as a result of learning that takes place within the family. Messages about sex, pleasure, and love have not always been positive. Therefore, many carry within their psyches negative ideas, thoughts, and perceptions about these things.

You all know this: Messages regarding the nature of sex, the enjoyment of sex, the frequency of sex, and the need for sex have all been complicated by parental attitudes and bias. It is unlikely that you will have matured within their environment without absorbing some of your parents' beliefs. Although their beliefs may not have served you, you had them nonetheless. They may not serve you now. You need to challenge them.

Ask yourself the following questions:

➤ What do I believe to be true today?

➤ Is it possible that what I learned is not right for me?

➤ Is it possible for me to let go of parental attitudes in response to my need to forge a more authentic sex life for myself now as an adult?

➤ Am I willing to do the work?

➤ Am I able to challenge what's not good for me anymore?

Sheila, age 49, is a schoolteacher who is willing to work hard on her repressions. For example, Sheila very easily identified having poor attitudes about sex that she clearly associated with her mother, who still gives her negative messages about it. Messages in the form of "I hope your husband doesn't make too many physical demands on you, if you know what I mean. . . . Men can be so nasty." Or, "If it hadn't been for your father's wandering eye, I would have been a much happier woman. He was always looking for something; I guess I wasn't giving it to him." Derisive comments like these are just the kind that suggest to a daughter that sex is just no good!

On the other hand, a younger woman in her late thirties told me her dying mother said this, "I know that you have never been satisfied with your husband; it doesn't take a brain surgeon to see that. I have noticed over the years how cold he is, how much he lacked warmth and affection. He couldn't be too loving in bed. Honey, find more for yourself in life. . . . Sexual connection is so important. You have many years ahead of you, don't sell yourself short."

"I think sex changed when I changed. It all went together," Alice, age 50, told me. She said that once she felt freed from her role as a dutiful daughter, she began to focus on her own needs. Once she did this, she began to realize how little sexual satisfaction she experienced in her marriage. In therapy, she started to examine how her inhibitions had contributed to the creation of this pattern. Eventually, Alice began to communicate her needs to her husband, and they began to explore different sexual positions, as well as increasing the general sensuality and intimacy in their relationship with increasing satisfaction.

Fortunately for Alice, her partner was willing and able to adjust to her newly emerging needs. Both people were willing to change.

The same held true for Neil, who lost his father when he was 49. As he put it, "I think I became more sexual after my father died because I felt more need for comfort and intimacy with my wife. The entirety of intimacy changed; no it became transformed after Dad died. I felt more suffering and more isolation which made me want to compensate by being close to someone else. . . . At least it all happened with my wife." Both Alice and Neil were lucky. They had partners who were flexible and willing to adjust to new needs in the marriage created by a dynamic change caused by parental loss.

Unfortunately, this is not always the case. In some marriages that are already problematic, parental death may become the catalyst for venturing beyond marriage for intimacy and sexual satisfaction and may even lead a person to decide to divorce. David, age 46, was in an unsatisfying relationship when his father died. His wife was cold and emotionally unresponsive. After the death of his father he found that he yearned for a closeness to compensate for his loss, and this emotional connection was not available with his wife.

As David puts it, "In contrast to my wife's unavailability, my secretary's every action all day long revolved around pleasing me. The atmosphere was ripe for the two of us. Sexually, we were great. I felt so comfortable with her and so sexually compatible, we were like two peas in a pod. I loved her as well. She was sexually giving and liked exploring things my wife would never consent to. There was a sexual openness I had never felt before." Although an extramarital relationship comes with its risks and complications, in David's case it was an important step toward a new kind of satisfaction.

Many people report a sexual liberation following parental death. In some cases, sexual fantasies that might have been seen as deviant by a traditional parent were finally able to be embraced and acted upon. Once-secret desires that would not have fit the family mold were now positive goals, and sexual activities that once seemed deviant were accepted as normal, pleasurable endeavors to be pursued. In general, for many people I worked with in my practice, a rich, full sex life became far more important once perceived parental approval was no longer an issue.

Changes in Lifestyle

Changes in lifestyle were reported by some orphaned adults. Inheritances helped many to have more financial freedom. Inheritances also helped make it possible for people to make career changes. Money certainly frees people. "I can finally go back to school and study law . . . ,"said one of my patients. "I left my profession after my father died, he wanted me do things his way, and now I don't have to do what he wanted me to do anymore."

Lifestyle changes may be as simple as an adult orphan saying to him- or herself, "Well, I'm tired of carrying those same 10 extra pounds Dad (or Mom) did, and now I'm going to start exercising and lose them." Another orphan who was exceedingly messy and disorganized precisely because the now-deceased parent was a compulsively neat person may decide to wise up and organize his or her life. Although these are all very healthy lifestyle changes, the shifts may be more varied and profound.

For example, one patient of mine who had had a particularly dominant father found that once her father passed away, she began to set limits and let others know when they had crossed the line both personally and professionally. Although she did not change her career or leave her marriage, she found a new freedom within herself that altered how she lived every aspect of her life. As she said to me, "I decided not to be a doormat any longer. It took time, but I got there."

For people who have been ambivalent about a life decision, the death of the parent offers an opportunity to resolve the situation, whether it be to decide to go ahead and have a child, adopt a child, leave a bad relationship, or make a career change. Sometimes people report that they were just going along with "the way things were," and then found that the jolt of parental death offered the incentive to take the step toward resolution.

It is important to note that the lifestyle changes I am discussing are not always part of coming to terms with orphanhood. Nor are important life decisions to be taken lightly or made precipitously.

However you experience lifestyle changes, small or large, quickly or more slowly, adult orphans do report that making a specific change not only helps in coping with their grief, but also works as a way of paying homage—honoring your loved one by taking a positive step into your own future. Making a change for the better is a metaphorical way of blessing the grave with flowers.

8

Your Life Your Way:
Embracing Possibility

As soon as you trust yourself, you will know how to live.
—*Johann Wolfgang von Goethe*

We have discussed the motivations that are driving you to change and to become your fullest self and the ways in which you can begin to go about realizing this goal. You have doubtless encountered some of the same experiences as the people I interviewed for this book have described. You are not alone in this process of reevaluation and renewal, and there is comfort to be had as you learn that others have had similar experiences to your own and used them to good purpose.

From Grief to Discovery

You have suffered through your own grief, and your experience of bereavement will continue to change and cycle with the passage of time. Your recovery process allows you to examine yourself and new directions you might take. You are ready to own your new identity, realizing that the old you no longer exists. The old you had parents, the new you does not. The old you was a child, the new you is a full adult.

Becoming the fullest *you* is your own adaptation to having no parents. By integrating lost aspects of your self into a new and transformed identity, the appropriate response to loss has evolved into gain. This is your parents' last and most enduring gift to you.

Will there be an end to grief? The answer is yes and no. As painful as it is to accept, there is no way to lose a loved one and ever completely get over it. One of the first battles in the field of bereavement counseling was deciding whether to call the stage of the grief process in which the bereaved started to feel better and rejoin life "acceptance" or "adaptation." At first, this stage was referred to as *acceptance*. When it became clear that no one truly "accepts" death—meaning that the natural instinct to deny death overshadows anything else—the term *adaptation* was chosen. Feeling or thinking you may never completely heal from your loss is common. It is not unusual to hear comments like the following:

> "It has been many years since the death of both of my parents, and I still miss them, wish I could talk to them, think about picking up the phone to call them, feel pain in my gut . . . but I go on with my own life."

> "I miss my parents, but I feel them around me and my children, and see them in my dreams."

> "My whole life is damn different. I cried plenty. Everything revolved around my mother. . . . With her gone, everything is just damn different. Hey, life's got to go on."

> "No matter what, no matter how bad they were, they were my parents, and I will think about them for the rest of my life."

> "Whenever good things happen to me the very first thing I notice is that I want to pick up the phone and call Mom."

> "Parents will always be there . . . in your memories, your dreams, your visions. Maybe they *are* waiting at the gate for you when you die, like some say."

In all, a new sensitivity and a new understanding are cultivated to transform the feelings of grief and loss. The time has come to claim both the depth of inner feeling associated with loss and the height of freedom that is released by this same loss. These feelings and realizations are to be your own personal discovery and they are as unique as you are.

Loving Them from Afar

Many believe that the parental relationship is never over, and research has added to this belief. Often people mention their desire to maintain a connection to the parent after death. These very important relationships seem to have a continuity that performs two functions. The continuity helps people with both their grief and the adaptation to their new life. Also expressed is the belief that the orphan will always be in "relationship" to the parent. Their tie to each other will exist, in some regard, forever, whether in waking or sleeping hours. Furthermore, there is an indication that, despite the loss of physical contact, contact does remain—emotionally, psychologically, biologically, mentally, spiritually, and through history and memory.

Feelings of connection to parents after death can serve us in several ways. One is through the internalization of parental behavior, which is part of the adaptation response. The second is through a process of identification that eventually allows the release of the actual person. Identification is a symbolic union based on the need both to hold onto the person and at the same time let go. Maintaining symbolic bonds with your deceased parents does not in any way minimize your ability to grow up and become yourself.

Embracing Life Force

Learning to metamorphose loss into gain is a process stimulated by creativity and life force. "The living have to go on living" is the watchword for all who have suffered loss and eventually return to live their lives. But what does this really mean? How do you accomplish such a goal? Human beings have within them a natural instinct to live that must be engaged at this point in the process. In addition, the recognition takes place that you have no other choice but to go on.

Here are some observations people have made about this crossroads in their lives:

"The death of someone you love and are close to is the worst thing that can happen to you, but hey, what are you going to do . . . you have to survive."

"It was returning to the things I loved to do that saved me from falling into a deep depression. I felt so abandoned when my parents were not here to protect me."

"There was a deep inner urge to get going in life, my time was running out."

One of the factors that makes parental death so daunting is the loss of innocence that accompanies this suddenly becoming grown up. The feeling of abandonment that people experience to varying degrees, and from time to time, is actually based on the fantasy and, for some, a partial reality that the parent can protect you from the dark, whatever the dark has come to mean for you.

This fantasy is powerful and lingers into adulthood unless it is surrendered through consciousness. As a child you were protected from the exigencies of life because your parents provided you with what was necessary for your survival. You needed to learn the skills of taking care of yourself. To become fully adult means you leave *all* yearning to be dependent on your parents behind, and you take full responsibility for *yourself.* This includes being true to yourself.

Transition into adulthood is typically thought of in chronological terms, you become an adult when you reach a certain age. Yet, this is often not the case. If nothing else, orphanhood will define you as a full adult because your parents' deaths have taken away your childhood and any ability for you to remain dependent on them. Now is the time to grow up. Now is the time for growth! Growth and life force are friends. One feeds the other. You have only to look within to find the urge to live, to grow, to develop, to mature, to transform.

If One Thing Is Possible, Anything Is Possible

As one of my patients said after becoming an orphan, "The sky is the limit." Or, anything you can imagine can be possible now. This is a time to create, think, plan, and take action. Change is possible, but change needs to be planned. Some changes will be spontaneous, others will not. One thing is clear, your new identity allows you to define yourself as a unified whole with access to parts that may be new and exciting.

Plans for the future should be well thought out and agreed upon by your spouse and/or children when necessary. These plans should be devised from a solid foundation, not impulsiveness or vulnerability without balance from the rational side of your being. Live with potential decisions for a considerable amount of time before plunging into behavior.

> Martha, age 60, remarked: "I was seriously shocked at my own reaction when my last parent died. I felt so alone. It was a very difficult time for me and my family. Yet, within time I was equally shocked by how good I felt because my freedom allowed me to take chances. I can remember talking to my best friend and I told her I felt as though I could do anything in the world I wanted. I almost felt mania as I described it.
>
> "As I began making plans for the things I wanted to do, like, build a house somewhere in the South, I understood that it was my fantasy I was living out. Was that okay, I wondered?"

Living out fantasies is certainly possible at any time in life, but certainly becomes desirable during the time of life when your parents are gone, and you are as free as you will ever be if you let yourself be.

A Time to Examine Fantasies

Sit down with your journal and examine your answers to the following questions:

What "chance" would you like to take?

Describe a fantasy from the earliest part of your life.

What was your attitude about it?

Think about that fantasy now. What do you presently think about it?

What would you like to do about this fantasy now?

Do you have a new fantasy about your life?

How can you turn this fantasy into a reality, now?

Do you have support from your friends regarding this fantasy?

What plan can you devise to make the fantasy real?

What time frame do you have for this action?

Remember: Always make changes in small increments, challenge your resistance, and support yourself for any positive progress. It is important to claim your successes, however small.

Change Over Time

The first two to three years after your parents die feel very different from the next several years. Most people obviously experience their greatest difficulty with loss immediately. But, life is long, and the rest of your life without your parents is ripe for change, introspection, and new beginnings.

> Carole, age 55, had this to say: "It has been 20 years since my father died, but only 10 since my mother died. As time goes on I still miss them both, and I remember them with a loving attitude. But, my life feels so different, even though I have adjusted to life without them, there is an inner strangeness that seems to never go away. It is an empty feeling. I will have it for the rest of my life I suspect. I am not always aware of it, but it is there and from time to time I feel it. However, the things I now do I would not be doing if they were still alive. For example, I moved and I left my career."

Jennifer, age 47, said: "When my last parent died, leaving me orphaned, I adjusted quickly. I was busy with my own family, my career, my husband's career, and really didn't think about "my orphanhood" as a transitional state. However, when the activity level quieted down in my own busy life, I did begin to sense many inner feelings, some of which made me uncomfortable, like depression, abandonment . . . maybe those feelings were there all along and I never noticed them."

What is the relationship between grief and time? Research suggests many ideas, the most predictable of which is that while grief subsides over time and the triggers for painful memories diminish, there is always a residue. S. L. Carter, in "Themes of Grief Work," has noted, "Grief seems to occur in 'waves' of intense pain which may be triggered many years after the death."[1] P. C. Rosenblatt, in *Bitter, Bitter Tears: Nineteenth Century Diarists and Twentieth Century Grief Theorists,* notes, "Over time the intensity of the feelings associated with the death changes very little, but what changes is that salient triggers grow fewer."[2] There is a reported absence of a significant correlation between grief and time which supports the notion that the grieving process is not always a strictly linear one.[3] The quotes that follow will bear this out.

Mark, age 52: "I never expected to still feel pain from time to time, so many years later. I think it is natural because so many other people feel the same way. A sound, a smell, music on the radio will suddenly make me cry."

Jack, age 49: "I respected my father and my mother. I am left with good memories. Over time I have felt more alone in the world, and I was surprised to see no end to my grief but I started reaching out to friends more for companionship and connection."

Stan, age 37: "If I had to describe the process of becoming orphaned, becoming myself and adjusting to the world without my parents in it I would say this: It has its highs, its lows, its pluses and its minuses. But, then, I am a math teacher."

Patricia, age 54: "It's curious, I feel both stronger and weaker each passing year. I am certainly totally independent now, self-sufficient. I rely on very few people to help me make decisions or to share my thoughts with. I do what I want. However, I still miss both of my parents and wish they were here to watch their grandchildren grow up."

Peter, age 36: "Freedom flows back and forth. Within me is a free spirit, but then I always check in with the part of me that is not, I consider both parts. But, I would say I am moving in the direction of doing more what my free spirit wants me to do."

Judith, age 57: "It is surprising to me how one day I can be driving down the street and suddenly burst into unprovoked tears at the thought of my mother or father."

Internalizing Parents

It is part of the bereavement process to internalize parts of your parents. Some people are surprised about the extent to which they happily state, "My mother or father did that," or "That is like my mother or father." These may be expressions, behaviors, attitudes, values. After so many years of becoming independent from parents, some adapting orphans are shocked to be so anxious to be "like Mom" or "like Dad."

Identifying with deceased parents provides comfort and maintains proximity to the parents after their deaths. As the previous comments have suggested, ties to parents continue long after the parents are physically absent. This identification allows you to continue to feel the ties: That is a powerful human need. Adopting the traits of parents is the expression of this identification. It is a natural occurrence and an aspect of coping with grief. This is part of how the legacy left to you by your parents is constructed.

Ultimately, there will be a change in the subjective view the bereaved has of the self, incorporating the "new me" and the parental aspects. This view, perpetually subject to more change, reflects more of the family history over time.

> Carole, age 60, remarked: "I took great comfort in the fact that as I aged I looked more and more like my mother, she was a pretty lady."

> Mary, age 53, said: "I was sad that as I moved into menopause, my mother was not present and someone with whom I could share. She never told me much about that time for her and my memory of how she coped is slight. I don't know if she had hot flashes or how she handled them. I do know she used hormone replacement . . . so I was not entirely distant from that part of her life."

The human condition thrives on energetic consistency. Those whom we love, we will always love and hold dear forever. Our histories are assured of continuation through this process, and our biological or social heritage depends upon such occurrences.

According to M. Moss and S. Moss, the "[d]eath of parents ushers in a sense of needing to reorganize the self as a way to deal with the profound impact of the loss. Personal growth does not demand a rejection of parental legacies but rather a selective integration of them into one's own value system."[4] I encourage you to feel comfortable with your natural tendency to enhance your own self with some part of either one of your parents, if not both.

Parental Legacy

Again, there is great comfort in creating parental legacies. Following are some comments regarding these comforts made by women about their mothers:

"The time immediately after my mother died was spent in mourning and coping with all my emotions. As time passed I began to look at myself for the ways I was acting like her, it didn't upset me, now it made me feel good to be like her."

"I noticed I began wearing my hair like Mom, first just like her, then the same color, but longer."

"I started using her things; all the feeling attached to her dishes gave me a feeling of continuity as I looked at them."

"I couldn't wear her clothes, but I loved wearing her jewelry, it made me feel close to her."

"I began hearing her voice in my own words. I was starting to sound like Mom, use her phrases . . . she lived on."

"I can remember how my mother would sit at her desk and pay bills. Eight years after she died I organized my own home office to look like hers. I felt more in control that way."

Men had this to say about their fathers:

"Dad always washed his hands at the kitchen sink before dinner. It is a ritual I watched with pride and have now copied."

"I noticed myself scratching my chin like Dad did."

"Dad always seemed to have a funny throw away expression, now I do the same thing."

"I see my father's face in the mirror when I shave; it's okay."

"I am more like my father than I ever would have admitted."

Family legacy lives on in behaviors, attitudes, values, traditions, biology, photographs. Observing photographs of lost parents is often painful. In time, this response can change and many have found great comfort in placing photos of their parents in places where they will see them every day, serving as a loving reminder of the ongoing bond they share with their parents.

THE REDISCOVERED YOU

In this lifelong process of growth and development, as you search for a place in the world that allows your real self to flourish, you remain vulnerable to the early and subsequent influences of your parents and other significant caregivers in your life. While it's true that by their early twenties most people arrive at conclusions—some tentative, some definite—regarding their own needs and interests, independent of the influences of others, it is not uncommon to rethink these issues again at various stages of development.

This includes midlife, the developmental stage at which orphanhood is most likely to occur. In midlife, for instance, divorce, remarriage, and career changes are common, and these types of life revisions, each powerful in its own right, are even more powerfully affected when you become an adult orphan. Orphanhood offers spontaneity and an opportunity for growth by creating a space in which the real self can navigate without the same conscious and unconscious influences from parents. The result is that your life takes on—or returns to—a more authentic shape. Your real self moves out of the shadows and into the light of your own needs, wishes, goals, and desires, and as it does, you experience a rush of satisfaction and passion for living that you may well have never before experienced.

Benefits to You of Returning to Your Authentic Self

- ➤ Feeling of congruence
- ➤ Feeling of completeness
- ➤ Feeling of contentedness
- ➤ Experience of having choice
- ➤ Feeling of consistency
- ➤ Feeling of connection
- ➤ Feeling of community
- ➤ Increased creativity

Congruence: the match between who you feel yourself to be on the inside and who and what you express.

Completeness: the feeling of wholeness you finally have achieved.

Contentedness: the joy that comes from full self-expression.

Having choice: many new choices are available.

Consistency: the benefits you experience as you witness that you have always been the same and the return to your true self, your center.

Connection: connection to your self and to your parent in death.

Community: the growing meaning of your relationship to others, nature, culture, community, life.

Creativity: the rediscovery of your creative nature.

Benefits to Others:

➤ Philanthropy

➤ Creative contributions

➤ Social/political contributions

➤ Family/relationships

➤ Children

Margarete, age 61: "Charity work became very important to me after Mom died. I donated many of her possessions to homeless shelters in my city. I felt gratitude about inheriting so much from her and wanted to share my wealth. How much does one need after all?"

Hal, age 56: "I had always entertained the idea of getting into politics. After Dad died, I ran for office in my town. I did it for both of us; he would have been proud, and it had been one of my dreams."

Carole, age 60: "Losing my parents left me without anyone else in my family. Being an only child I was now without any remaining biological tie. Naturally my need for contact grew, and I began involvements in many social groups, from within the community to my place of worship."

Creativity Springs Forth

Many who have experienced this loss agree upon one thing: losing their parents sent them back to themselves, and one of the first and most gratifying aspects discovered was their creative sides. Among people in their forties, fifties, and sixties there is consensus that their creativity suffered more than almost anything else in their childhoods. Whether the message emanated from school, society, or parents, it was loud and clear: "Be productive"; "Play it safe"; "Make smart choices"; "Make a good living"; "Do what I didn't do"; "Make something out of yourself." It is not likely that the parental message was "Follow your creative instinct." Free of your parent's voice, you can now follow your creative instinct. What does it tell you to do?

> Connie, age 48, had this to say: "Now that my father is dead I don't have to practice law. He wanted to be a lawyer, I didn't. I wanted to be an artist. I have always felt the happiest when I was drawing; I should have studied art. Well, it's never too late, I am going back to school next year. I have waited this long; all my children are grown and its time for me!"

Responsibility

You have transitioned into a time of your life where your personal responsibility is at its fullest. You are more adult now than ever, as your childhood has been taken by the deaths of your parents. You can accept this, fight it, and/or make the most out of it. Taking full responsibility for your life now is a significant option, and means:

➤ Making your own decisions

➤ Handling family or personal affairs previously belonging to parents

➤ Being responsible for a remaining ailing sibling, stepparent, other family member

➤ Acquiring skills of money or property management

➤ Recognizing when to hand over the responsibility to someone else if you realize you are unable to be efficient

➤ Personal responsibility—being responsible for yourself in every way

Each of you will have your own idea of what personal responsibility means for you. The concept is that you handle all of your own feelings, problems, conflicts, and needs, which for some will be a learning process. This process will take time and will ebb and flow of its own accord.

How much time you will need is going to be different for all of you. What might work for you the first year after losing your parents will not work in the fourth year. Or, it might be the case that a problem you have in the fifth year didn't exist in the second year. For example, a man, age 54, took over his father's business when his dad died. The first three years were satisfying, but by the fifth year he was advertising to sell the business and was ready to move forward with his own life.

To be responsible means to accept fully the consequences of all of your actions. This is actually what is most beautiful about being "the full adult." There is no one to answer to. No one should be questioning you. You can be taking care of others. You should be making decisions for those who cannot. You are fully in the leadership role now.

Contributions

This is the time in your life that is ripe for making a contribution to something or someone. I am not discussing financial contributions. I am talking about giving of yourself; contributing to the world, in whatever way possible. If you feel you were born to do something special, now is the time to do it. If your life has purpose, express it now.

Depending on your age at the time of being orphaned and the status of your own family, you may have time to devote to something other than yourself. If your children are still young, this may not be possible for you. However, if they are grown, it is the time for you to realize that "deep-rooted sense" of wanting to put back into the community, come to life.

As we have seen, researchers verify my own personal finding that orphanhood ignites a process of life reassessment that results in learning how and what you value in life. The more life means to you, the more the inclination for wanting to give back. The more you value life, the more you are inspired to give. Many of those who have lost their parents begin to participate in charities, social organizations, community activities, church or synagogue, schools, and such. Sometimes, orphans become involved in groups formally associated with their parents.

John, a 49-year-old CEO educated on the East Coast, returned to the institution where his father had been a professor to volunteer after his father's death. He felt a duty to maintain a connection to the place for both his father and himself. "I am serving a dual purpose," he said. "I am giving of myself and I am staying connected to my father by working in his old environment."

Again, the idea of maintaining connections to deceased parents arises. It is safe to say that despite what freedom comes after their deaths, or whatever opportunities you take for your own individual advancement it is unlikely you will be moved to forget about them after they are gone. Rather, keeping their memory alive and loving is important. For those of you whose relationships were poor, I refer you back to Chapter 2, where I discuss the importance of "forgive, forget, and repair."

Remember:

➤ You are not alone.

➤ There is gain after loss.

➤ You have a real self waiting to be discovered.

➤ Your real self has always been there.

➤ It is full of passion and creativity.

➤ Use the forces of passion and creativity to your own advantage.

➤ If possible, mend broken parental relationships.

➤ Live life to the fullest when you choose to be free.

➤ Share your gifts with the world.

➤ Teach others to be true to themselves.

➤ Learn to love yourself.

➤ Live the rest of your days expressing your true self.

It is a fact: Life as an orphan *becomes about individuality,* it is about who you are apart from the goals, needs, and demands of your parents, and in learning this, it can *also* be about who you are independent of the goals, needs, and demands of *others* in your life. Your life can truly become *about you* for the first time. How you will change is open; the sky is the limit. Your changes can be sudden, in direct relationship to your needs. What you have suppressed is what you need to connect with and rediscover.

Because it is a time for individuality, you will vary from everyone else in terms of how you reevaluate your life. Your siblings, who become orphans when you do, will not follow the identical path; a friend who coincidentally loses his or her parent when you do will go on a different journey too. This truth about how we experience loss and rediscovery is one of the great beauties of this stage of development: It is at once full of possibility and creativity, yet offers the most potent of individuality when it comes to choices. You do not need to follow any path other than the one that unfolds in front of you, making itself clear to—and through—your heart.

This is the final gift from your parents: They have given you the gift of loss so that you can accept and forgive, discover and be whole, reclaim and create. With their final act they will allow you to rediscover yourself in all of your uniqueness. This is no small token; give this gift the credit it is due by continuing, now, on your path toward creating, experiencing, and reclaiming the self that is awaiting only a word from you to be set free.

It takes courage to grow up and become who you really are.—E. E. Cummings

Endnotes

CHAPTER 1

1. Colin Murray Parkes, *Studies of Grief in Adult Life* (London: Tavistock Publishing), 1972, p. 121.
2. Ibid.
3. Elisabeth Kubler-Ross, *On Death and Dying* (New York: Macmillan), 1969, p. 9.

CHAPTER 2

1. Ros Weston, *Loss and Bereavement: Managing Change* (Malden, MA: Blackwell Science), 1998, p. 6.
2. Jane Littlewood, *Aspects of Grief and Bereavement in Adult Life* (London: Tavistock), 1992, p. 16.
3. Maxine Harris, *The Loss That Is Forever* (New York: Penguin Books USA), 1996, p. 14.
4. C. S. Lewis, *Surprised by Joy* (San Diego, CA: Harcourt Brace), 1956, p. 21, quoted in Maxine Harris, *The Loss That Is Forever* (New York: Penguin Books USA), 1996, p. 14.
5. Ros Weston, *Loss and Bereavement*, p. 7.
6. Jane Campbell, Paul Swank, and Ken Vincent, "The Role of Hardiness in the Resolution of Grief," *Omega*, 23(1), 1991, p. 61.

CHAPTER 3

1. Robert A. Neimeyer, *Lessons of Loss: A Guide to Coping* (New York: McGraw-Hill), 1998, p. 91.
2. Carl Jung, *Modern Man in Search of a Soul* (Florida: Harcourt), 1933, p. 104.
3. Colin Murray Parkes, "The First Year of Bereavement: A Longitudinal Study of the Reactions of London Widows to the Death of Their Husbands," *Psychiatry*, 33, 1971, p. 444.
4. Catherine M. Sanders, "A Comparison of Adult Bereavement in the Death of a Spouse, Child and Parent," *Omega*, 10, 1980, p. 303.
5. Miriam Moss and Sidney Moss, "The Impact of Parental Death on Middle-Aged Children," *Omega*, 14(1), 1984, p. 65.
6. Robert S. Weiss, "Loss and Recovery," *Journal of Social Issues*, 44(3), 1988, p. 37; and *Attachment in Adults: The Place of Attachment in Human Behavior* (New York: Basic Books), 1982, p. 173.

7. John Bowlby, *Attachment and Loss: Vol. 1, Attachment* (New York: Basic Books), 1969, p. 79.
8. Colin Murray Parkes, *Bereavement* (New York: International University Press), 1972, p. 52.
9. Miriam Moss and Sidney Moss, "The Impact of Parental Death on Middle-Aged Children," p. 66.
10. Ann R. Bower, "The Adult Child's Acceptance of Parent Death," *Omega,* 35(1), 1997, p. 69.
11. Andrew E. Scharlach and Karen I. Fredriksen, "Reactions to the Death of a Parent During Midlife," *Omega,* 27(4), 1993, p. 307.
12. Miriam Moss and Sidney Moss, *The Death of a Parent in Midlife: Coping Strategies,* edited by R. A. Kalish (Newbury Park, CA: Sage Publishing), 1989, p. 121.
13. Marvin Eisenstadt et al., *Parental Loss and Achievement* (Madison, CT: International University Press, Inc.), 1989, p. 35.
14. Ibid., p. 174.

CHAPTER 4

1. Robert S. Weiss, "Loss and Recovery," *Journal of Social Issues,* 44(3), 1988, p. 38.
2. John R. Jordan and Eugenia S. Ware, "Feeling Like a Motherless Child: A Support Group Model for Adults Grieving the Death of a Parent," *Omega,* 35(4), 1997, p. 361.
3. Ibid., p. 362.
4. Miriam Moss and Sidney Moss, "The Impact of Parental Death on Middle-Aged Children," *Omega* 14(1), 1984, p. 66.
5. *Diogenes Laertius: Lives of Eminent Philosophers,* translated by R. D. Hicks (Cambridge, MA: Harvard University Press), 1938.
6. Andres Malraux, *Man's Fate,* reissue (New York: Knopf) 1989.
7. Anonymous poem reprinted with permission of the author.
8. Miriam Moss and Sidney Moss, *The Death of a Parent in Midlife: Coping Strategies,* edited by R. A. Kalish (Newbury Park, CA: Sage Publishing), 1989, p. 121.
9. Colin Murray Parks, *Recovery from Bereavement* (New York: Basic Books), 1983.
10. George H. Pollock, "The Mourning Process and Creative Organizational Change," Plenary Session Post-Presidential Address, given December 20, 1975, at the Midwinter Meetings of American Psychoanalytic Association, New York, NY, p. 18.
11. Andrew E. Scharlach and Karen I. Fredriksen, "Reactions to the Death of a Parent During Midlife," *Omega,* 27(4), 1993, p. 307.

CHAPTER 5

1. *Webster's New World Dictionary* (Second College Edition), (New York: Simon & Schuster), 1984.

CHAPTER 6

1. Miriam Moss and Sidney Moss, "The Impact of Parental Death on Middle-Aged Children," *Omega* 14(1), 1984, p. 68.
2. Thomas Moore, *Care of the Soul* (New York: Harper Collins), 1992, p. 35.
3. Marvin Eisenstadt et al., *Parental Loss and Achievement* (Madison, CT: International University Press, Inc.), 1989, p. xiii.
4. Sidney Moss, R. L. Rubinstein, and Miriam Moss, "Middle-Aged Son's Reactions to Father's Death," *Omega*, 34(4), p. 259.
5. Ibid., p. 269.

CHAPTER 7

1. Robert S. Weiss, "Loss and Recovery," *Journal of Social Issues,* 44(3), 1988, p. 46.
2. Ibid., p. 47.
3. Debra Umberson, "Marriage as Support or Strain: Marital Quality Following the Death of a Parent," *Journal of Marriage and the Family,* 57, August 1995, p. 709.
4. Ibid., p. 709.
5. Ibid., p. 710.
6. Ibid., p. 710.
7. Ibid., p. 711.
8. Barbara Bartocci, *Nobody's Child Anymore* (South Bend, IN: Sorin Books), 2000, p. 98.

CHAPTER 8

1. S. L. Carter, "Themes of Grief Work," *Nursing Research,* 38, 1989, p. 354.
2. P. C. Rosenblatt, *Bitter, Bitter Tears: Nineteenth Century Diarists and Twentieth Century Grief Theorists* (Minneapolis: University of Minnesota Press), 1983, p. 70.
3. S. L. Carter, "Themes of Grief Work," p. 356.
4. Miriam Moss and Sidney Moss, "The Impact of Parental Death on Middle-Aged Children," *Omega,* 14, 1984, p. 67.

Bibliography

Akner, Lois. *How to Survive the Loss of a Parent: A Guide for Adults*, William Morris and Co., Inc., New York, 1993.

Angel, Marc D. *The Orphaned Adult: Confronting the Death of a Parent*, Insight Books, Human Sciences Press, New York, 1987.

Balk, David E., and Laura C. Vesta. "Psychological Development During Four Years of Bereavement: A Longitudinal Case Study," *Death Studies*, 22, 23–41, 1998.

Bartocci, Barbara. *Nobody's Child Anymore; Reclaiming Purpose and Passion*, Sorin Books, Inc., Notre Dame, IN, 2000.

Benjamin, Jessica. *The Bonds of Love: Psychoanalysis, Feminism, and the Problem of Domination*, Pantheon Books, New York, 1988.

Bettelheim, Bruno. *A Good Enough Parent*, Random House, New York, 1987.

Bower, Anne. "The Adult Child's Acceptance of Parent Death," *Omega*, 35(1), 67–96, 1997.

Bowlby, John. *Attachment and Loss, Vol. III Loss: Sadness and Depression*, Harper Collins, New York, 1980.

Bradshaw, John. *Bradshaw On: The Family*, Health Communications Inc., Florida, 1988.

Brooks, Jane. *Midlife Orphan: Facing Life's Changes Now That Your Parents Are Gone*, Berkeley Books, New York, 1999.

Calhoun, Lawrence, and Richard Tedeschi. "Positive Aspects of Critical Life Problems: Recollections of Grief," *Omega*, 20(4), 265–272, 1989.

Campbell, Jane, Paul Swank, and Ken Vincent. "The Role of Hardiness in the Resolution of Grief," *Omega*, 23(1), 53–65, 1991.

Csikszentmihalyi, Mihaly. *The Evolving Self*, Harper Collins, New York, 1993.

Douglas, Joan Delahanty. "Patterns of Change Following Parent Death in Midlife Adults," *Omega*, 22(2), 123–137, 1990.

Edmonds, Sarah, and Karen Hooker. " Perceived Changes in Life Meaning Following Bereavement," *Omega*, 25(4), 307–318, 1992.

Eisenstadt, Marvin, Andre Haynal, Pierre Rentchnick, and Pierre de Senarclens. *Parental Loss and Achievement*, International Universities Press, Inc., Madison, CT, 1989.

Gamino, Louis A., Kenneth W. Sewell, and Larry W. Easterling. "Scott and White Grief Study—Phase 2: Toward an Adaptive Model of Grief," *Death Studies*, 24, 633–660, 2000.

Harris. Maxine. *The Loss That Is Forever*, Penguin Publishing, New York, 1996.

Hillman, James. *Suicide and the Soul*, Spring Publishing Inc., Texas, 1976.

Hogan, Nancy S., Daryl B. Greenfield, and Lee A. Schmidt. "Development and Validation of the Hogan Grief Reaction Checklist," *Death Studies,* 25, 1–32, 2001.

Horowitz, Marti J., Janice Krupnick, Nancy Kaltreider, Nancy Wilner, Anthony Leong, and Charles Marmar. "Initial Psychological Response to Parental Death," *Archives of General Psychiatry,* 38, March 1981.

Jordan, John, and Eugenia Ware. "Feeling Like a Motherless Child: Support Group Model for Adults Grieving the Death of a Parent," *Omega,* 35(4), 361–376, 1997.

Klass, Dennis. "John Bowlby's Model of Grief and the Problems of Identification," *Omega,* 18(1), 13–30, 1987.

Krementz, Jill. *How It Feels When a Parent Dies,* Alfred A. Knopf, New York, 1981.

Kubler-Ross, Elisabeth. *Death: The Final Stage of Growth,* Prentice Hall, New York, 1975.

Lindemann, Erich. *Symptomatology and Management of Acute Grief,* Read at the Centenary Meeting of The American Psychiatric Association, Philadelphia, PA, May 15–18, 1944. From the Department of Diseases of the Nervous System, Harvard Medical School, and the Department of Psychiatry, Massachusetts General Hospital.

Malinak, Dennis P., Michael F. Hoyt, and Virginia Patterson. "Adults' Reactions to the Death of a Parent: A Preliminary Study," *American Journal of Psychiatry,* 136(9), 1152–1156, September 1979.

Markova, Dawna. *Reclaiming Purpose and Passion: I Will Not Die An Unlived Life,* Conari Press, Berkeley, CA, 2000.

Masterson, James. *Search for the Real Self,* Macmillan Inc., New York, 1990.

Miller, Alice. *Drama of the Gifted Child: The Search for the True Self,* Harper Collins, New York, 1990.

Moore, Thomas. *The Original Self,* Harper Collins, New York, 2001.

Moore, Thomas. *Care of the Soul,* Harper Collins, New York, 1992.

Moss, Miriam S., and Sidney Moss. "The Impact of Parental Death on Middle-Aged Children," *Omega,* 14(1), 65–75, 1983–1984.

Moss, Miriam S., and Sidney Moss. *The Death of a Parent in Midlife: Coping Strategies,* edited by R. A. Kalish, Sage, Newbury Park, CA, 75–89, 1977.

Moss, Sidney Z., R. L. Rubinstein, and M. S. Moss. "Middle-Aged Son's Reactions to Fathers Death," *Omega,* 34(4), 259–277, 1996.

Myers, Edward. *When Parents Die: A Guide for Adults,* Penguin Books, New York, 1987.

Neimeyer, Robert A. *Lessons of Loss: A Guide to Coping,* McGraw-Hill, New York, 1998.

Nietzsche, Friedrich. *On The Genealogy of Morals: Ecce Homo,* Random House, New York, 1967.

Parkes, Colin Murray, and Robert S. Weiss, *Recovery from Bereavement,* Basic Books Inc., New York, 1983.

Pollack, George H. "The Mourning Process and Creative Organizational Change," *Journal of the American Psychoanalytic Association,* 25, 3–34, 1977.

Rando, Therese A. *Treatment of Complicated Mourning,* Research Press, Champaign, IL., 1993.

Rochlin, Gregory. "Loss and Restitution," *The Psychoanalytic Study of the Child,* 8, 288–309, International Universities Press, New York, 1953.

Sanders, Catherine. *Surviving Grief and Learning to Live Again,* John Wiley and Sons, New York, 1992.

Sanders, Catherine. "A Comparison of Adult Bereavement in the Death of a Spouse, Child and Parent," *Omega,* 27(4), 307–319, 1993.

Scharlach, Andrew, and Karen I. Fredriksen. "Reactions to the Death of a Parent During Midlife," *Omega,* 27(4), 307–319, 1993.

Secunda, Victoria. *Losing Your Parents, Finding Yourself: The Defining Turning Point of Adult Life,* Hyperion Press, New York, 2000.

Stone, Hal, and Sidra Winkleman. *Embracing Ourselves,* Devorss and Co., Camarillo, CA, 1985.

Umberson, Debra. "Marriage as Support or Strain? Marital Quality Following the Death of a Parent," *Journal of Marriage and the Family,* 709–723, 1995.

Umberson, Debra, and Meichu D.Chen. "Effects of a Parent's Death on Adult Children: Relationship Salience and Reaction to Loss," *American Sociological Review,* 59, 152–168, 1994.

Viorst, Judith. *Necessary Losses: The Loves, Illusions, Dependencies and Impossible Expectations That All of Us Have to Give Up in Order to Grow,* Fawcett Gold Medal, Ballantine Books, New York, 1987.

Weiss, Robert. "Loss and Recovery," *Journal of Social Issues,* 44(3), 37–52, 1988.

Wheeler, Inese. "Parental Bereavement: The Crisis of Meaning," *Death Studies,* 25, 51–66, 2002.

Wortman, Camille B., and Roxane Cohen Silver. "The Myths of Coping with Loss," *Journal of Consulting and Clinical Psychology,* 37(1), 1989.

Index

About the Author

Shari Butler, Ph.D., is a psychotherapist with more than 20 years of clinical experience. For the past several years, she has been devoted to working with people who have lost their parents. She received her doctorate at the California School of Professional Psychology and her master's degree at UCLA. Dr. Butler lives in Connecticut. She moved there with her family after the death of her mother.